HASHTAG HINDU

NOT A SERMON. NOT A LECTURE. JUST DHARMA, DECODED

RAJIV MENON

CONTENTS

HASHTAG HINDU — SYNOPSIS

Why are we Hindu? What does it even mean today?

For many young Indians—especially those living outside Bharat—this isn't just a spiritual question. It's cultural, personal, even political. *Hashtag Hindu* steps into that uncertainty, not as a preacher or purist, but as a bridge between generations, geographies, and Google searches.

This book doesn't deliver lectures. It sparks conversations. It doesn't water down Hinduism, but it doesn't fossilize it either. With warmth, wit, and sometimes irreverent honesty, *Hashtag Hindu* unpacks festivals, rituals, gods, temples, caste, and mythology—through the lens of Kerala's Hindu traditions and the modern diaspora's identity crisis.

Using everything from SpongeBob to the Smritis, it helps readers navigate Sanatana Dharma with cultural fluency, not just religious literacy. The tone may be cheeky, but the intent is sincere: to spark curiosity, connection, and continuity.

Whether you light a lamp daily or can't remember the last time you prayed, this book is for anyone trying to figure out what Hinduism means in a world of memes, migration, and modernity. It's not just a book about belief—it's a user manual for belonging.

Purpose & Audience

Hashtag Hindu is for:

- The millennial and younger generation Indians (especially diaspora)
- Curious readers raised in multicultural or secular environments
- Families seeking a fun yet respectful way to explain rituals and values
- Educators and cultural organizations wanting modern Hindu material

Author Intent

The author — an Indian-born cultural commentator with Kerala roots — wrote this book to decode Hindu traditions for a new generation who don't just want religion; they want meaning, agency, and relatable context. Hashtag Hindu is not about making Dharma "cool." It's about showing that it already is — and has been — for thousands of years.

FOREWORD TO HASHTAG HINDU

By Dr. Shashi Tharoor

As a grandfather to young Indian-Americans growing up in a world of TikTok trends and touchscreen temples, I often wonder how they will come to understand the faith and culture that shaped their ancestors. Will they see Hinduism as a living philosophy or a dusty relic? Will they feel pride in its pluralism, or confusion at its complexity? Will they ask questions—or simply swipe past?

This book, *Hashtag Hindu*, offers answers. Not in the form of sermons or scholarly treatises, but through memes, metaphors, and a tone that speaks directly to the digital generation. It is witty, warm, and wise—a rare combination in any genre, let alone one that tackles the vast and intricate terrain of Sanatana Dharma.

I intend to gift this book to my grandchildren in America—not as a textbook, but as a companion. A primer that meets them where they are, and gently nudges them toward where they might want to go. It is a book that doesn't preach, but provokes thought. That doesn't simplify, but clarifies. That doesn't mock tradition, but makes it intelligible—even delightful.

The author, with Kerala roots and a cosmopolitan sensibility, has pulled off something remarkable: a guide to Hinduism that is unapologetically modern without being reductive. From the very first pages—where Twitter meets Tilak and glossary meets giggle—we are invited into a world where ancient ideas are reframed for contemporary minds. The Upanishads are not diluted, but decoded. The Trimurti are not trivialised, but translated into archetypes that resonate with today's youth.

Each section of the book is a journey. In *Hinduism 101 – But Make It Epic*, we encounter the cosmic architecture of Dharma through storytelling that is both reverent and relatable. The Goddess is not just divine—she's your inner supermom. Devas and Asuras are not distant deities—they're psychological forces we wrestle with daily. This is not theology as dogma, but philosophy as lived experience.

In *Spiritual Wi-Fi Zones*, we travel from Bharat to Kerala, exploring the regional textures of Hindu practice. Here, caste is not brushed under the carpet—it is confronted with history and humour. Colonial legacies are unpacked, and Kerala's unique blend of tantric, tribal, and temple traditions is presented with clarity and curiosity. For diaspora readers, this section is especially valuable—it shows that Hinduism is not monolithic, but richly diverse.

The chapters on temple architecture and sacred geometry are among my favourites. They reveal how rituals and spaces are not arbitrary, but intentional, designed to align body, mind, and cosmos. The idea of temples as "energy hubs" rather than mere monuments is beautifully explained, and the field guide to Kerala's major shrines is both informative and inviting.

In *Myth-Taken Identities*, we see how Hindu myths are not just stories, but symbolic maps of the human condition. Family rituals, menstruation taboos, and festival customs are demystified with a blend of science, sensitivity, and satire. This is precisely the kind of unpacking that young readers need—not to reject tradition, but to understand it on their own terms.

The final chapters—*Power Moves* and *Dharma Downloads*—are a call to action. They show how dance, martial arts, and nature-based rituals are not just cultural artifacts, but spiritual technologies. The closing message, "Kalki Is You," is a powerful reminder that Hinduism is not about waiting for saviours, but awakening the hero within.

What makes *Hashtag Hindu* truly special is its tone. It is never condescending, never cynical. It respects the intelligence of its readers, even as it entertains them. It is written with humility and humour—two qualities that are often missing in religious discourse. And it is inclusive: welcoming to sceptics, seekers, and believers alike.

For members of the Indian diaspora—especially those raised in multicultural or secular environments—this book is a bridge. It connects them to their heritage without guilt or pressure. It offers context, not commandments. It shows that Hinduism is not about blind belief, but about inquiry, introspection, and inner growth.

As someone who has spent much of my life trying to explain India to the world—and sometimes to Indians themselves—I see *Hashtag Hindu* as part of a larger cultural project: making our traditions accessible without making them simplistic. It is a book that belongs in classrooms, living rooms, and yes, even on coffee tables. It is a book that can spark conversations across generations.

To the author, Rajiv Menon, I offer my congratulations. To the readers, I offer my encouragement. And to my grandchildren, I offer this book—with love, hope, and the belief that understanding one's roots is not a burden, but a blessing.

May *Hashtag Hindu* inspire a new generation to explore their faith with curiosity, confidence, and compassion. May it remind us all that tradition is not a chain—it is a compass: one that can guide us to the most important destination, the one within our hearts and minds.

— *Shashi Tharoor*

New Delhi, September 2025

PRAISE FOR HASHTAG HINDU

"Your refreshing work creatively connects current generations with antiquity. Kids these days know more about Hogwarts than Hastinapura? No problem for you. You've drawn the analogies that keep the Hindu history — both cosmic allegorical and actual — alive and thriving. A fun read."

— *Easan Katir*

"Rajiv Menon has nicely put together a composite view of Sanatana Dharma, aka Hinduism in a language well understood by our younger generation. While avoiding the cliche of traditional texts, the core principles and concepts are introduced to attract the curious among the younger generation. I hope this book will lead many of our youth to study Sanatana Dharma in more detail and enrich their lives by practice thereof."

— *Prem Chandran*

"They say laughter is the best medicine, and Rajiv Menon has skillfully used humor and witty storytelling to bring Indic wisdom to life. Some may not agree with every joke or logic, but I urge readers to experience the book before judging. Even a smile gained along the way makes the effort worthwhile."

— *Vibhuti Jha*

PREFACE

From Twitter to Tilak: Reconnecting Roots

This Isn't a Guilt Trip. It's a Field Trip.

Let's be real: in a world where your fridge texts you and AI writes your homework, who has time to sit cross-legged in incense while someone tosses flowers at a statue?

Meanwhile, there's been this treasure chest of stories, festivals, philosophies, and gloriously dramatic gods—just waiting. Think Room of Requirement, except with more coconuts.

This book? It's your Marauder's Map to Hinduism—told through my Kerala-centered experiences. But I promise, whether you're Malayali or not, you'll find the journey relatable.

No sandal-beating nostalgia trips here. Instead, a backstage pass to a culture where:

- Elephants have résumés
- Rituals come with beats and feasts
- And gods pull plot twists that could humble Marvel

If you grew up outside India, you may know more about Messi than Mahabharata. Consider this your Portal of Po—to the legends your grandparents meant to share before Wi-Fi hijacked dinner.

We decode the "why," not just the "what":

- Why light a lamp?
- Why are gods blue and multi-armed?
- Why do festivals feel like raves with food stalls?

Peek behind the curtain and you'll see: these aren't relics. They're superpowers—timeless, vivid, and designed to outlast trends.

And for every generation:

- Millennials → your translator.

- Gen Z → your decoder ring.

- Gen X → your shortcut to re-rooting.

- Gen A (next up) → your bedtime stories, explained before Alexa takes over.

So no, this isn't just a book.

It's your cultural GPS. Unlock it—and you won't look at your roots the same way again.

ACKNOWLEDGMENTS

To the curious version of me—50 years ago.

You didn't have all the answers. Heck, you didn't even know the questions. But you kept poking around between rituals, temples and Amar Chitra Kathas.

If I had a time machine (or cosmic shortcut), I'd sit you down with some payasam and say:

"You are not broken for feeling disconnected. You are not weird for questioning things. You don't need Sanskrit or perfect shlokas to belong."

The chaos has rhythm. The gods have logic. And your doubts? They were the beginning of clarity.

This book is for you—my first skeptic, first seeker, and first spiritual side-eye.

A heartfelt shoutout to the brilliant millennial voices, sharp Gen Z family members, and trusted friends who stayed actively engaged— even in the final moments before publication. The millennials helped me fine-tune the focus of this book, so its voice resonated most naturally with their generation, while still leaving room for others to connect. To the family and friends who patiently proofread draft after draft (sometimes through truly painful iterations) and helped me refine both tone and content, your persistence and perspective carried this work across the finish line. Your insights, truth bombs, and well-timed mic drops shaped the last pieces of this book, and for that, I remain deeply grateful. 🧡

Namaste to the philosophers of Reels and Shorts—the 30-second sages whose insights packed more punch than a theology class. This book carries your spark—filtered through my head but lit by your fire.

But mostly—dear younger me—this one's yours.

May your tilak stay un-smudged and your prasadam always warm.

⚠️ DISCLAIMER: SACRED HUMOR AHEAD

This book blends scripture with satire, and weaves together myths, metaphors, and spiritual truths—with a side of Harry Potter, Avengers, Kung Fu Panda, and SpongeBob. (Blame my kids for turning movie night into multiverse madness.) It's written with deep respect for Hindu philosophy—and an even deeper belief that asking questions, laughing at our quirks, and connecting ancient ideas to Netflix, noodle bowls, or jelly fishing isn't sacrilege. It's survival.

While the title focuses on Kerala Hindus, only the rituals and some traditions are region-specific. The core ideas of Sanatana Dharma apply across Bharat and beyond—whether you're chilling in Chennai, vibing in Varanasi, or Zooming in from Zurich. Think of this book as spiritual Wi-Fi from my corner of the dharmic universe—hoping others recognize the signal and find familiar apps (a.k.a. rituals) running in their own lives too.

This book is brewed from personal reflections, temple life, family wisdom, field notes, and generous servings of Nickelodeon and sci-fi fandom —because that's what the next generation might read.

If you came looking for a sandal-wearing, sit-still-and-chant commentary... this probably isn't it. But if you're ready to explore Sanatana Dharma with curiosity, cultural pride, and a little cosmic mischief—welcome to the party.

If at times the tone slips into sounding like I'm talking to a toddler or a preteen, that's intentional — it's written for you, millennials, to pass on with ease to your own children.

One Last Note

I had help writing this—not from elves, ghosts, or ghostwriters—but from friendly neighborhood digital AI sidekicks. They helped zhuzh up the visuals, wrangle emojis, massage tones, and hang in there for my 3 a.m. ramblings under jetlag.

That said, every idea, interpretation, analogy, and final call is my own. No robot wrote this. If anything, here sounds weird, wise, or wildly both—that's 100% me.

All references to gods, sages, avatars, or rituals are symbolic, metaphorical, and remixable. No deities were harmed in the making of this manuscript.

You're welcome. Or... sorry.

Now grab your popcorn, charge your chakras, and let's get spiritually sarcastic.

⌚ How to Use This Book (Without Losing Your Mind)

Read This First: Surf the Dharma Wave Without Crashing

Whether you're a practicing Hindu, a curious explorer, or someone who just thought "that elephant god looks cool"—you're in the right place.

First, Hit Reset:

Forget the Bollywood drama, guilt trips, or spiritual pressure. This isn't about dogma. It's:

- Less "Bow or else," more "Why and how?"
- Less mythology dump, more "Wait... that actually makes sense."
- Less sermon, more logic.

Read It Like This:

- Start with the Hinduism Primer
- Chapters 1 to 4 = your Dharma foundation
- Then pair and play: → 7 + 8, → 9 + 9 3/4, → 10 to 12, → 17 to 19
- The rest? Freestyle. Flip to whatever sparks joy or existential FOMO

Some chapters end with a Field Guide—a bite-sized scroll of takeaways for busy brains.

What's Inside?

- Hinduism 101 for the "Why Tho?" generation
- A hoverboard-style time-travel tour of Kerala
- Caste, customs & cosmic grandma logic
- Science vs superstition in a logic smackdown
- And the ultimate upgrade: seeing the sacred without the melodrama

Decode the intent. Ditch the nonsense. Keep the magic.

Last Step: Flip to the Glossary

Seriously. It's not optional—it's survival gear.

Prologue: Why This Book, and Why Now?

🧠 PROLOGUE: WHY THIS BOOK, AND WHY NOW?

(Spoiler: It's Valliamma's Fault)

Before we dive into chapters, emoji-packed field guides, and temple trivia, I need to introduce you to the woman who unintentionally co-wrote this book: Valliamma—my grandmother, who should have been called Ammamma, but ended up with her unique title thanks to a young aunt for whom she was a Valliamma (mom's older sister)...and a crew of older cousins who made it stick by copying her like it was the next big trend.

I grew up in Kerala, in a setting where Hindu traditions weren't something you Googled—they were just... life. You didn't ask why someone was lighting a lamp or chanting a mantra—you just joined in, or pretended to mutter something with the elders, mostly because someone shouted your name from the puja room and you were too scared not to.

But Valliamma? She wasn't your typical cuddly, lullaby-singing grandma. She was fierce, funny, and unapologetically wise. Think Professor McGonagall meets Aunt May, with a touch of Master Shifu. She could out-recite a panel of Namboodiris in any shloka fest or mantra-off—extemporaneously—while calmly dipping Britannia biscuits in coffee.

Her brain was basically a shloka vault. She had a sixth sense for catching ritual slip-ups and a storytelling style that made even the Mahabharata feel like a Netflix original with five plot twists per episode. And when she read out loud—she didn't just read, she performed. Her voice, tone, and energy could make even SpongeBob sit still and listen.

Here's the plot twist

As I've grown older, I've realized I don't agree with everything Valliamma believed in. She was sometimes a little too chill about how Hinduism was interpreted—or should I say, rebranded—for wide-eyed audiences being sold spiritual clickbait.

She had a forgiving heart —even when she gave airtime to so-called "truths" and anubhavams (personal spiritual experiences) that, to me and my cousins at our family Hogwarts, felt like rehearsed conjuring—cleverly packaged to win reverence, favors, or both. It was clear they were more marketing than mantra.

But here's the thing: she always showed up with full presence. Whether lighting a lamp, tying a thread, or explaining a verse from a crumbling old book—she did it with mindfulness and purpose. That's the energy I try to bring into everything I do.

Not blind acceptance, but curious engagement.

Not "chant in sync," but "think in sync".

This book? It is part memoir, part survival guide, and part "wish-I-had-this-before-I-tried meditating like Po—totally Zen on the outside, totally confused on the inside".

It is packed with cultural decoding, bold questions, and stories that help Hinduism make sense in a world run on Wi-Fi, burnout, and a million tabs open—both in your browser and your brain.

And one thing you should know up front:

The views and interpretations in this book are entirely my own, shaped by how I, as a Kerala Hindu, have experienced, questioned, and made sense of Sanatana Dharma over the years.

See It as a jailbreak for your inner spiritual system—breaking you out of outdated scripts and handing you a fresh lens.

- Take what resonates
- Question what feels off
- Keep what makes you feel grounded.

Just like Valliamma—if she'd grown up with Google, streaming, and a SpongeBob-level sense of timing—would've wanted.

That's because, Sanatana Dharma?

It's not some relic in a glass case.

It's a living tradition.

It evolves. It breathes.

And yeah, it totally deserves your attention.

🌟 WHO IS THIS BOOK FOR?

(Besides You, Reading This with One Eyebrow Raised)

Hey there, Millennials 👋

Yes — you. The one who once downloaded ringtones on a Nokia, survived Orkut, and now juggles work calls, side hustles, and maybe even parenting. This book is for you.

You grew up in the in-between — half analog, half digital. You remember floppy disks and Netflix, Harry Potter and Marvel, forwarding chain mails and writing LinkedIn posts. You've questioned school systems, career ladders, fast fashion, and probably your family's ritual of boiling rice on Pongal. But there's still a quiet voice — maybe your grandma's, maybe your own — that sometimes wonders:

"Why do we light that lamp? Who's the goddess on the fridge magnet? What does any of this mean?"

This book won't guilt you into blind faith. Think of it as your crash course + cultural comeback + dharmic decoder. Inside you'll find logical hacks for rituals, metaphysical takes on mantras, and enough philosophical plot twists to make even Marvel look tame.

Here's the catch: you're not just decoding this for yourself. You're also a future parent, mentor, or myth-buster-in-chief for the next round — let's call them Gen Aloha. They'll grow up with AI lullabies, bilingual Alexa, and maybe even digital deities in AR. If we don't pass down our stories, they might assume Sanatana Dharma is just a yoga studio or the latest crypto coin.

So, whether you're here to reconnect, decode, or avoid saying "Ask Ammamma," this book is your field guide to the sacred, the silly, and the seriously underrated roots of your heritage. And who knows — your Gen Aloha might thank you someday for keeping the flame alive, literally and metaphorically.

PS: While this book speaks first to Millennials, it's also a decoder ring for curious Gen Z'ers and rediscovering Gen X'ers (from one of your own). And if you're from an entirely different spiritual squad, think of this as your backstage pass to one of the world's oldest, most misunderstood traditions. No head-bobbles required.

 GLOSSARY:

Hindu Terminology Glossary (Alphabetical)

A quick reference guide to help you decode common Hindu terms used throughout this book.

Adharma – Actions or behaviors that go against dharma, unrighteousness or disorder.

Amavasya – New moon day, considered spiritually significant for rituals and ancestral offerings.

Ayurveda – Ancient Indian system of holistic medicine based on balance between body, mind, and nature.

Bhagavan – A reverential title for God or the Supreme Being.

Bhagavathy – A term for the Goddess, especially in Kerala, representing Shakti in her many forms.

Bhakti – Devotion or love directed toward a personal deity.

Chandan – Sandalwood paste used in rituals for cooling, fragrance, and sanctity.

Dharma – Righteous duty, moral law, or one's true path in life.

Gopurams – Towering, ornate gateways characteristic of South Indian temple architecture.

Guru-Shishya Parampara – The teacher–student lineage through which knowledge is passed down.

Karma – The principle of action and consequence; what you do comes back to you.

Kumkum – Red vermillion powder, often applied on the forehead or offered in rituals as a symbol of energy and auspiciousness.

Mantra – Sacred sound or phrase believed to carry spiritual power and transform consciousness.

Moksha – Liberation from samsara; ultimate freedom and union with the divine.

Nilavilakku – The traditional Kerala brass oil lamp, lit at dusk and dawn as a symbol of divine light.

Payasam – Sweet pudding made of rice, milk, and jaggery; a staple dessert of Kerala festivals.

Pookkalam – Floral designs laid out on the ground during Onam in Kerala, symbolizing welcome and celebration.

Pooja – Ritual act of worship offered to a deity, involving offerings, chants, and devotion.

Pournami – Full moon day, often associated with fasting, worship, and heightened spiritual energy.

Pradakshina – Circumambulation around a deity or temple, symbolizing alignment with cosmic order.

Prasadam – Blessed food offered to a deity and later shared among devotees.

Pratishtha – The consecration ritual by which divine presence is invoked into a temple idol.

Sadya – A grand Kerala vegetarian feast, usually served on a banana leaf during festivals.

Samsara – The cycle of birth, death, and rebirth.

Samskaras – Life-cycle rituals in Hinduism, from birth to death, marking spiritual and social milestones.

Shakti – The divine feminine energy and cosmic power behind creation and life.

Shikharas – The rising spires or domes of North Indian temples.

Shloka – Verses or hymns from sacred texts, often recited as prayers.

Thiruvathira – Kerala festival honoring Parvati's devotion to Shiva, marked by women's rituals and dance.

Utsavam – Festival or celebration, often centered around temples and community gatherings.

Vastu – Traditional Hindu system of architecture and spatial design, aligning structures with cosmic principles.

Vibhuti – Sacred ash, usually from temple fire rituals, applied to the forehead as a reminder of purity and impermanence.

A Survival Guide a.k.a. How to Speak Hashtag Hindu without calling Tech Support

- Vibe—The general feeling, mood, or energy. "This temple *vibes*."
- Flex—A humble brag. Showing off something cool—spiritually or otherwise.
- Lowkey/Highkey—*Lowkey*: subtle. *Highkey*: loud and proud. "Low-key love Ganesha. High-key obsessed with Kali."
- Ghosted—When someone disappears on you (emotionally or textually). "Like that one deity you stopped praying to… and never texted back."
- Woke—Socially and spiritually aware. Not just awake— *awakened*.
- Cringe—Second-hand embarrassment. "Explaining karma like it's instant coffee? Cringe."
- Canceled—Done. Over. Usually something outdated or problematic. "Caste-based pride? Canceled."
- Mood—Deep relatability. "Krishna chilling with a flute? Mood."
- Drop—Release of new stuff. "Chapter 12 just dropped, and it's fire."

Glow-Up—Transformation for the better. "That Shiva statue after abhishekam? Total glow-up."

Thirst Trap—A post meant to get attention. "Hanuman shirtless in posters? Literal thirst trap."

It's giving…—Describing vibes or essence. "It's giving divine feminine."

🙇 Not me [doing X]—A funny, self-aware confession. "Not me praying for good marks and then bingeing Netflix."

Acronym Decoder

OG—Original Gangster

LOL—Laugh Out Loud (not Lots of Love, Aunties 😅)

BCU—Bharat Cinematic Universe

BRB—Be Right Back

OMG—Oh My God / Gosh / Ganapati 😮

TBH—To Be Honest

TL; DR—Too Long; Didn't Read (summary time!)

EDM—Electronic Dance Music

NPC—Non-Playable Character

FOMO—Fear Of Missing Out

JOMO—Joy Of Missing Out (Zen upgrade to FOMO)

RIP—Rest In Peace (or "RIP my attention span during 3-hour bhajans")

DLC—Downloadable Content—bonus material. Think: Appendixes, Dharma Downloads, or extra temple trivia.

TBA/TBD—To Be Announced / To Be Determined

CEO of [X]—The best at something. "You're the CEO of diyas, bro."

GOAT—Greatest Of All Time ("Hanuman is the GOAT of loyalty.")

📘 Hinduism Primer (for the Abrahamically Accustomed)

First up:

There. Is. No. Such. Thing. As. Hinduism.

Yep, mind = blown. Even most Hindus don't realize this plot twist.

Origin Story:

Long before anyone shouted "Avengers, Assemble!", the land was called Bharatvarsha or Sapta Sindhu (Land of Seven Rivers).

Then the Persians mispronounced Sindhu as Hindu, Greeks renamed the river Indus, and boom —India.

The Chinese? Tianzhu. The Japanese? Tenjiku. Translation: "Heavenly Land".

But the belief system itself? Not Hinduism. The OG name is Sanatana Dharma—The Eternal Way. No brand. No founder. Just cosmic flow.

Still, for simplicity's sake (and because we're not rewriting Wikipedia today), we'll roll with Hindu and Hinduism. Think of it like calling Thor's hammer just... "hammer".

Wrong Universe?

If you're expecting one sky-God with rules, thunderbolts, and eternal judgment—sorry, wrong cinematic universe. Hinduism isn't a monologue. It's a multiverse.

Here, gods are metaphors, not monarchs. Rituals are rhythms. Salvation? Optional.

Why It's Confusing (But Worth It)

Imagine trying to impress one all-seeing God who acts like Dumbledore + Nick Fury + Master Shifu + Squidward. Exhausting, right?

Now, enter Hinduism: No single cosmic overlord.

We've got thousands of deities, all vibing in divine chaos—Ganapati with snacks, Saraswati with pens, Shiva meditating, Kali ready to rage.

Surprisingly, it's not chaos. It's customizable spirituality.

Choose your vibe. Switch your path. No lightning bolts if you skip Monday prayers.

Wait—No Gods?

In the Western sense? Zero.

Our "gods" are cosmic functions:

- **Brahma creates**
- **Vishnu sustains**
- **Shiva transforms**

Think Big Bang + evolution + entropy, explained in Sanskrit.

They're not sky beings. They're the Avengers of energy, ethics, and emotion.

And the Goddess? Not floating in clouds. She's your mom—nurturing, fierce, wise. Feminine energy = foundational, not optional.

Why the Cow?

No, she doesn't grant wishes.

She gave ancient India milk, butter, dung, fuel—zero waste.

Basically, the original sustainability icon.

Second only to mother's milk in digestibility. Science, not sentiment.

No Conversions. Just Vibes.

Hinduism is open-source spirituality.

No missionaries, no holy wars, no door-to-door salvation sales.

Truth, if it's real, doesn't need marketing.

Many paths. One mountain. Walk yours.

So, What Is It?

Not a religion in the Western sense.

More like a living playlist of stories, symbols, and seasonal wisdom.

You don't "follow" it. You flow with it.

And yes—spirituality goes better with biriyani.

Then, Who Is a Hindu?

A Sanatani or Hindu is anyone who steps into the cosmic playlist called Sanatana Dharma and grooves to it in their own style.

Atheist? No problem. Agnostic? Totally get you. Spiritual-but-not-religious? We understand Basically, a Hindu is one or all of the below:

- Open-source seeker
- Player in a multiverse
- Practitioner of rhythms, not rules
- Born into or drawn into the eternal flow a.k.a Sanatana Dharma
- Not a member, but a traveller
- Eco-friendly realist
- Story collector

Section 1:

🔱 Hinduism 101 —But Make It Epic

Chapter 1:
What Even Is Hinduism?
(Spoiler: It's More Than Just
Temples and Incense)

Chapter 1: What Even Is Hinduism?

🕉 Sanatana Dharma: The OG Eternal Life Philosophy

Okay, so we already said Hinduism isn't a one-god-fits-all deal. Let's go deeper: Sanatana Dharma isn't just old—it's eternal. Literally. Like cosmic Wi-Fi.

Hinduism isn't your typical "founded-in-500-BC-by-some-guy-on-a-hilltop" kind of religion. It doesn't have one founder, one holy book, or a universal dress code. In fact, calling it 'Hinduism' is kind of a modern thing—the original term is Sanatana Dharma, which means "the eternal way." Sounds like the title of a fantasy novel, right? Except this one has mantras, meditation, metaphysics, and the occasional monkey god —think more 'Po finds inner peace' than 'founder on a hilltop.'

Karma, Rebirth, and the Cosmic Escape Room

At the center of Hindu thinking are four big ideas:

- Dharma—Doing what's right, even when Wi-Fi is down and no one's watching.
- Karma—What goes around, comes around.
- Samsara—The cycle of birth, death, and rebirth.
- Moksha—The ultimate level-up: breaking free from the cycle and merging with Brahman.

Basically, life is like a giant escape room. Your mission? Collect karma like power-ups, follow your dharma like a true kung fu master, and unlock Moksha like the game's final boss level.

Vedas, Verses, and Epic Universe Lore

You thought your school textbooks were big? Hinduism's got volumes.

- Shruti— "Heard" wisdom, like divine downloads: the Vedas and Upanishads.
- Smriti— "Remembered" epics like the Ramayana, Mahabharata, and Puranas.

These texts weren't stored in the cloud—they were memorized and passed down through chanting.

The Bhagavad Gita? A spiritual TED Talk on a battlefield. Arjuna = confused warrior. Krishna = cosmic life coach.

Pick Your Deity, Pick Your Vibe

The divine comes in many forms; it's a spiritual multiverse.

Shiva (Zen transformer), Vishnu (protector), Durga (cosmic queen), Ganesha (problem-smasher) —> all are avatars of one truth, regardless of whether you're a Shaivite, Vaishnavite, Shakta, or Smarta. They're all valid.

Hinduism 2.0: Still Glowing After 5,000+ Years

Hinduism isn't just old scrolls and mantras. It is timeless advice for modern life.

You can chant, meditate, dance, do yoga, or just ponder existence—it all counts.

TL; DR?

Hinduism = lifestyle full of quests, upgrades, and mystical side missions.

No Sanskrit PhD required; just curiosity and maybe a wand (or chopsticks).

📜 Myth Buster Scroll: Hindutva—Voldemort Vibes or Vibranium Shield?

Hindutva: —An easy Guide to Understanding Hindutva—Beyond the Hashtags

So, with this new take on what Hinduism is and who a Hindu is, what then is Hindutva? This term has gained notoriety since circa 2004. First off, don't let anyone confuse you about what Hindutva truly stands for; there are many forces actively spreading misleading narratives about its meaning.

What media propagates:

Let's start with how Hindutva is usually seen on the internet, in news circles, or in your high school debate group:

- Hindutva ≠ Hinduism. Hinduism is a spiritual buffet—yoga, Vedanta, karma, bhakti, chill. —Hindutva = Political, a more aggressive alter ego. Like a Hindu Hulk, but with a press release and a WhatsApp army.
- The Core Narrative: According to critics, Hindutva wants India to be Hindu-first. Not spiritually, but culturally and politically. This has triggered concerns about minorities, secularism, and turning India into a saffron-only BCU.
- It's got squad associations: Frequently tied to groups like RSS, BJP, and VHP; often labeled the Slytherin House of Indian politics (which is unfair to both Slytherin and history, honestly).

The Controversy Snap (yes, Thanos-style):

Critics say:

- It's exclusionary.
- It's Islamophobic.
- It rewrites history as if it were fan fiction.

Supporters say:

- It is a comeback—not a conquest.
- It is about civilizational pride, not dominance.
- It is the Desi equivalent of Wakanda saying, "Never again will we be colonized or marginalized."

The Truth? Hindutva = Dignity, Not Domination. It was a term popularized by Savarkar in his 1923 book "Hindutva: Who is a Hindu?" In this work, Savarkar describes it as a socio-political idea about national identity, unity, and cultural pride rooted in Sanatana Dharma.

After Independence, India tried to be Professor X—fair, rational, and inclusive. But many Hindus felt cheated. India's version of secularism was defined unfairly like this:

- Hindu temples = Government property —The State controls Hindu temples but not churches or mosques.
- Hindu culture = Mocked as backward. Hindu festivals are regulated, but minority events get VIP treatment.
- Hindu rights = Subject to 'don't offend anyone else' clauses. Hindu history is often told through the lens of colonial rulers or Marxist ideologies.

Hindutva, in this light, isn't Voldemort. It is more like Captain India picking up the cultural shield after generations of being told to "keep it down." It showed up like a Dharma Guardian saying: "Hey! We have been polite. We have been patient. But we matter too."

If you are Hindu and unsure where you stand—don't be gaslit into thinking pride = hate.

- If being woke means knowing who you are,
- Then Hindutva, at its best, is your cultural shield—not your political prison.

And remember: "With great Dharma comes great responsibility."

Chapter 1 Field Guide: What Even Is Hinduism?

Sanatana Dharma Not 'Hinduism' originally—means 'The Eternal Way'. No single founder, no fixed rulebook.

Origins of 'Hindu' Comes from 'Sindhu' river—Persians called the people beyond it 'Hindus'.

Dharma Doing what's right, even when no one's watching.

Karma What you do comes back around—cosmic cause and effect.

Samsara Cycle of birth, death, and rebirth—yes, maybe even as a squirrel.

Moksha Ultimate escape—breaking the cycle to merge with Brahman (infinite divine).

Shruti & Smriti Heard & remembered texts. Think Vedas, Upanishads, Mahabharata, Ramayana.

Many Gods, One Truth Shiva, Vishnu, Devi, Ganesha—choose your vibe, same divine Wi-Fi.

Hinduism Today Yoga, rituals, inner peace—flexible, mindful, timeless.

TL;DR Hinduism = ancient wisdom + spiritual freedom + epic stories. No Sanskrit degree needed.

CHAPTER 2:
THE BIG THREE

BRAHMA, VISHNU, SHIVA

VISHNU'S REMIX PLAYLIST (A.K.A AVATARS)

Chapter 2: The Big Three and Vishnu's Remix Playlist (a.k.a. Avatars)

Previously on Sanatana Dharma...

You unlocked karma combos, leveled up through dharma, and nearly escaped samsara. Now, it is time to meet the squad running the cosmic dojo. This isn't mythology. It is an ancient multiverse of divine mentors and moral missions.

Part 1: The OG Cosmic Trio — Po, Dumbledore, and Hulk Walk Into a Universe

If the universe had a behind-the-scenes team like the Avengers, here's who is running the show:

- Brahma—The Cosmic Starter/Professor Dumbledore

Brahma is like Dumbledore at the moment of creation — full of ideas, long beard, and bursts of wisdom. He writes the magical blueprint (a.k.a. the Vedas) and fires the starter spell that launches reality. He is the guy who kicks off the plot but exits before Act 2 — kind of like a wise NPC who coded the game, then logged off.

- Vishnu—The Dharma Defender/Po Meets Captain America

Vishnu is the soft-spoken OG minimalist who saves worlds with style and barely raises his voice, and steps in only when the system glitches. Like Po after inner peace training, he holds it all together with balance, compassion, and the occasional superpowered avatar switch-up. He has the consistency of Captain America, but with cosmic flair and fewer shield throws.

- Shiva—The Cosmic Reset Button/Hulk x Snape Energy

Shiva is where chill meets chaos. He meditates like Po, mastering the Wuxi Finger Hold, but when transformation time comes, he goes full

Hulk-mode in dance form. Not evil—just misunderstood, like Snape with rhythm. He doesn't destroy for fun; he resets the universe so the whole band can start a new track.

- Shakti—The Power Behind It All/SpongeBob's Boundless Energy

Without Shakti, the rest are just powered-down action figures. She is the divine spark, the energy juice, the chaos coordinator who flips between nurturing goddess, fierce warrior, and spiritual Wi-Fi. She is the ancient equivalent of SpongeBob's unlimited optimism mixed with Kali-level confidence.

Part 2: Vishnu's Avatar Multiverse—Evolution, Dharma, and Divine DLC

Now that you have the big picture of life (a.k.a. Vishnu as the cosmic present), let's dive into one of Sanatana Dharma's most misunderstood —and most genius—concepts: the Dashavatara.

Dasha-Avatara = 10 avatars.

 "Why 10?"

Why the 10 Commandments? Why 10 avatars of Vishnu? Why not 9? Or 11? Or a surprise bonus round? Because nine feels incomplete. Eleven feels like a sequel nobody asked for. Ten is cosmic Goldilocks: just right.

Also, humans love the number ten. We have ten fingers, ten toes, and apparently a divine obsession with rounding things off neatly. The ancient Hebrews got 10 sacred laws on stone tablets (like an OG iPad), and Hindus? We got Vishnu dropping in across time with 10 power-packed avatars—each one a moral reboot when humanity goes off the rails.

But these aren't random cameos. The Dashavatara (literally, "ten avatars") follow an epic arc—from fish to warrior monk to apocalypse hacker.

And unlike the Commandments, which tell you what "not" to do, Vishnu's avatars show up and do. Action speaks louder than rules. So, buckle up: from aquatic rescues to demon smackdowns, this chapter isn't just mythology—it's Vishnu's ultimate highlight reel.

Okay, so avatars are not just cosmic superhero skins. They're also the oldest metaphor for evolution ever told—like Darwin, before Darwin could spell "natural selection".

Ancient Indian thinkers somehow narrated the journey of life from the ocean to human intellect long before fossils started receiving fan mail. Let's break it down like a cosmic Pokémon evolution chart—but with deeper meaning and a moral compass:

1. Matsya (The Fish) — (Life beginning in water)

The Flood Evader. When the world was drowning (literally), Matsya swam in to save the ancient Vedas and humanity's future—think Noah's Ark but make it desi. He reminds us:

Knowledge must be protected, even when everything else sinks.

2. Kurma (The Tortoise) — (Marine to Amphibious evolution)

The Stabilizer. During the legendary ocean churning (Samudra Manthan), Kurma became the steady base to support Mount Mandara. A cosmic tortoise-turned-tripod, teaching us:

When life gets turbulent, be the calm foundation others can stand on.

3. Varaha (The Boar) — (Amphibious to Mammalian)

The Earth Lifter. When Earth was kidnapped and drowned by a demon, Varaha dove into the cosmic waters, tusked it up, and saved the day. Moral of the story?

Even when Dharma is buried by chaos, the resilient Varaha shows it can be dug out and raised, no matter how deep it sinks—a lesson in resilience.

4. Narasimha (The Man-Lion) — (Evolution of Neanderthal mammal)

The Neanderthal of Dharma—This avatar needs a slightly longer explanation

Half-man, half-lion, and 100% loophole glitch in the system. In the grand Dashavatara-to-evolution metaphor, Narasimha = Neanderthal —the raw, emotional, instinct-fueled stage where survival gets personal.

Enter Hiranyakashyap—the cosmic tyrant with unbeatable cheat codes:

- No man or beast could kill him
- Not by day or night
- Not indoors or outdoors
- Not with weapons

Basically, evil.exe was unkillable.

But life finds a way.

The most famous saying in martial arts is, "No matter how tough you think you are, there's always someone tougher."

Typically, Vishnu (the essence of life) upgrades the system. No rage, no drama—just divine loophole hacking. The great leveler that life is, a being appears as a better-skilled warrior, challenges Hiranyakashyap, and

- appears at twilight (not day, not night)
- bursts out of a pillar (not inside, not outside)
- uses claws (not a weapon) and
- rips injustice apart to protect a loyal devotee.

This is evolution with a side of righteousness. When the rulebook is rigged, Dharma rewrites the code.

Narasimha is the cosmic reminder that even in the wildest chaos,

- Good adapts. Good evolves. Good survives.

This was not just survival of the fittest. It was survival of the fairest.

5. Vamana (The Dwarf) —This avatar also requires a bit of an explanation

The Homo Sapiens Era—When Brain > Brawn

Welcome to the Homo Sapiens update in the Dashavatara evolution lineup—the dawn of intelligence, strategy, and complex questions that leave even kings speechless.

Mahabali wasn't your average King. He was a benevolent overachiever —adored by his people, and so impressive that even the so-called divine ideals (read: gods with egos and control issues) started sweating.

With unmatched generosity and cosmic ambition, Mahabali's empire expanded across horizons (metaphorically across Heaven, Earth, and the Oceans)—basically, he hit the universal real estate jackpot.

And he did it not through fear or force, but through sheer dharmic swag and people-first policies. He gave his all and was ready to give even more.

But when someone gets that good, the system starts glitching. And the godly beings? Well... they called for a patch update.

Enter Vamana—the "vertically-challenged" monk with the brain of a strategist and the vibe of someone who knows exactly what he's doing.

He walks into Mahabali's court with zero flex, asks for just three steps of land —and the king, being the giver he was, says:

"Of course, little guy. Take it."

Except... plot twist:

Vamana requests real estate in the sky, in the ocean, and on earth. The depth of this question made Mahabali realize that he cannot give "everything". (again, metaphorically). A poetic power move

Let's break it down:

- Vamana didn't fight Mahabali.
- He outwitted him.
- He dropped a philosophical truth bomb:

"Even generosity has limits. Even kings have ceilings. Even dharma needs a reset sometimes."

But here's a spicy thought 🌶:

A Brahmin boy showing up to "humble" the most dharmic king ever? Smells a bit like a divine PR stunt to re-establish Brahmin superiority, doesn't it?

6. Parashurama (The Warrior Sage)

When Brahmins Go Full Battle Mode.

I have always side-eyed this avatar like, "Really? That's it?" Sure, it's a great story, but I could never quite figure out what made it avatar-worthy. So, bear with me while I try to make sense of a divine role that—on the surface—feels more "Wait, what?" than "Whoa, cosmic power move."

When the whole varna system starts glitching—especially with power-hungry kings abusing their role—someone's got to rage-quit the peace.

Cue: Parashurama—a peaceful shloka-reciting Brahmin's son and a woodcutter, who absolutely loses it when a Kshatriya king pulls the dumbest move ever:

Stealing their cow—the family's one source of sustenance, respect, and survival.

And just like that, it's Ax-first, ask—later mode.

This isn't your average woodcutter. Parashurama grabs his divine weapon—the ax equivalent of Mjölnir —and goes full "holy avenger" on not just one king, but 21 entire generations of Kshatriyas. Talk about an overcorrection.

But here's the twist:

He's a Brahmin. He's doing warrior stuff. And now he's sending a new message:

"Spiritual power + Physical dominance = Top-tier Brahmin unlocked."

Sound familiar? Yep—yet another Brahminic patch update, where intellectuals get to be warriors too... and no other varna gets the cross-over bonus.

- Extreme? 100%.
- Justified? Debatable.
- But strategically written into the lore? Highly likely.

Parashurama showed that when dharma breaks down, the script sometimes bends toward violence in robes.

Whether that's divine justice or ancient spin-doctoring... well, you decide. (See Chapter 7: "Caste and Curious" for more politely roasted Brahminical drama)

7. Rama (The Ideal King)

The Dharma Dude. Prince. Exile. Bridge-builder. Demon-slayer. One-woman man. Rama's life is a dharma playbook, filled with honor, sacrifice, and the ultimate rescue mission (Sita!) if Krishna is your witty older cousin, Rama is your noble elder bro.

8. Balarama (The Plow Wielder)

The Strong Silent Type. Krishna's elder brother and Earth's bodyguard. With his mighty plow, he tills through ignorance and grounds you in tradition. Not flashy, but solid — your inner anchor when life's vibes go haywire.

9. Krishna (The Divine Strategist)

The Trickster-Philosopher flute player by day, warrior-philosopher by night. Krishna breaks rules to save higher rules, offers the Gita in the middle of a battlefield, and delivers karma mic drops like no one else. Also, the original prank king.

10. Kalki (The Future Warrior)

Kalki isn't some distant, sword-swinging savior riding in from the skies. He is the awakening within you—the part that refuses to stay silent when dharma is violated.

In an age where chaos looks like clickbait and injustice scrolls by unnoticed, you are the one meant to rise.

- Your white horse = courage, will, honor.
- Your sword = awareness + action.
- And the battlefield? Real life.

So, Kalki is not coming. Kalki is becoming. And that becoming? It's happening to you. Right now. You are here to finish what the avatars started. (see Chapter 19: Kalki is You for more)

📜 TL; DR?

- Matsya (Fish)—🌊 Life Begins in Water
- Kurma (Tortoise)—🐢 Amphibious Support Mode
- Varaha (Boar)—🐗 Mammalian Muscles Arrive
- Narasimha (Man-Lion)—🦁 Neanderthal Roars In
- Vamana (Dwarf Sage)—🧙 Intellect Awakens
- Parashurama (Ax Sage)—🪓 Class Crossovers Happen
- Rama (The Ideal King)—👑 Dharma in Flesh
- Balarama (Grounding Force)—🌾 The Tanky Support Class
- Krishna (Strategic Statesman)—🎻 The Mastermind Avatar

CHAPTER 3
FROM HALOS TO HORNS—
MEET YOUR INNER CONFLICT TEAM
(Devas, Asuras & Rakshasas)

Chapter 3: From Halos to Horns— Meet Your Inner Conflict Team

Ever feel like SpongeBob characters are secretly managing your emotions? One moment you're bubbly, helpful, radiating sunshine like SpongeBob. Then you're Squidward—salty, eye-rolling, done with humanity. And suddenly, Plankton shows up—rage-y and ready to torch the world over a missed text.

Turns out, ancient Hindu mythology saw this inner chaos coming.

They named it:

- Deva—your pure, dharmic side (a.k.a. SpongeBob mode)
- Asura—your intense, ambitious side (Squidward in boss mode)
- Rakshasa—your wild, no-filter chaos monster (Plankton vibes)

So yeah... your mood swings? Totally mythological.

Let's break down your cosmic inner crew:

✨ The Devas—Your "Good Vibes Only" Mode

Think of Devas as the universe's wellness warriors: calm on the outside, thunderstorm-ready inside.

Role: Keep order, protect Dharma, bless humans

HQ: Svarga (the celestial spa-meets-war zone)

Famous Faces: Indra, Agni, Varuna, Lakshmi

Superpower: Righteous discipline

Catchphrase: "Stay in dharma, kids."

They are not just sparkly and nice. Devas are you when you are calm, kind, and trying not to snap during rush hour traffic.

😤 The Asuras—Overachievers with a Chip on Their Shoulder

Asuras started out equal to Devas—until ego and ambition hit "beast mode."

Role: Cosmic disruptors, challengers of the status quo

HQ: Yoga retreats, throne rooms, and dramatic shadows

Famous Faces: Mahabali, Hiranyakashipu, Ravana

Superpower: Ambition without brakes

Catchphrase: "I just want... everything."

They are not evil. They are you when your to-do list takes over your soul and you are ready to debate your dog for dominance.

👹 The Rakshasas—Chaos Gremlins With Issues

Rakshasas = your untamed side when you are hangry, dramatic, and one Wi-Fi dropout away from disaster.

Role: Stir up trouble, test heroes, crash rituals

HQ: Haunted forests and drama forts

Famous Faces: Ravana (yes, he holds dual citizenship), Kumbhakarna, Vibhishana

Superpower: Raw emotion dialed to 100

Catchphrase: "RAAWR. Also... snacks?"

They are not always villains—just your inner mess with a megaphone and no bedtime.

Plot Twist: Who is Really the Villain?

It is not that simple.

- Some Devas are problematic (Indra, we are looking at you)
- Some Asuras are noble (Mahabali = gold standard)
- Some Rakshasas have a heart (Vibhishana for the win)

These aren't just mythical labels—they are your inner crew:

- Devas = Your wise side (meditates, calls grandma)
- Asuras = Your driven side (hungry for growth)
- Rakshasas = Your emotional side (hangry tantrums)

Final Tip: Don't Kill the Chaos—Balance It

Let your Deva lead with clarity.

Channel your Asura into passion and purpose. Let your Rakshasa rest (or feed them before they burn your group chat).

The battle isn't out there. It's in here.

And the goal isn't to pick sides. It is to master the squad.

Field Guide: Chapter 3—From Halos to Horns: Inner Conflict Team (Devas, Asuras, and Rakshasas)

DEVAS—YOUR WISE MODE

- 🧘 Devas = Dharma squad, cosmic rule-followers.
- ⚡ Indra, Agni, Varuna = Sky, fire, and water guardians.
- 🌙 Shine bright, stay calm, bless others.
- 🕉️ Catchphrase: 'Stay in dharma, kids'.

ASURAS—THE AMBITIOUS OVERACHIEVERS

- 💼 Smart, powerful, but a bit dramatic.
- 👑 Mahabali, Ravana, Hiranyakashipu = iconic but flawed.
- 🏅 Stubbornness = superpower (and flaw).
- 🔥 Inner Asura = ego when it is running the show.

RAKSHASAS—CHAOTIC ENERGY, UNFILTERED

- 👹 Loud, emotional, often misunderstood.
- 👯 Rage + fear + selfishness = inner Rakshasa.
- 😴 Kumbhakarna = nap king. Vibhishana = the one with a conscience.
- 🍪 Last-cookie guilt? Total Rakshasa moment.

THE REAL SECRET

- ⚪ These are not just mythological characters—they're YOU.
- 🩷 Deva = mindful of you.
- 🚀 Asura = greedy, ambitious youth.
- 🗡️ Rakshasa = messy you up on a bad day.

BONUS WISDOM

- ⚖️ Good and evil are complex.
- 😈 Some Devas misbehave (ahem, Indra).
- 🌞 Some Asuras shine (Mahabali is a hero in Kerala).
- 💗 Some Rakshasas have a heart (Vibhishana = conscience goals).

YOUR INNER TEAM MANAGEMENT PLAN

- 🧘‍♂️ Meditate like a Deva.
- 💪 Build like an Asura.
- 🔥 Vent like a Rakshasa—just don't rage-post.
- ⚖️ Balance is the real superpower.

Chapter 4:
The Goddess—
Your Inner Supermom

CHAPTER 4: THE GODDESS — YOUR INNER SUPERMOM

Let's talk about the real MVP of Hinduism. Not just the blue-skinned gods or the cosmic snake rides —but the power behind everything.

Ever wondered why so many Hindu deities are goddesses? Why does one ride a lion, another floats on a lotus, and one looks terrifying but protects the innocent?

This isn't just mythology.

It is the ultimate reverence to the life-giver—the mother, reflected in divine form.

Who Is the Goddess, Really?

In Hinduism, the Goddess is called Devi or Shakti, which literally means power. She is the energy behind the universe —the force that gives life, protects it, and helps it grow.

In short? She is pure mom energy:

- Teaches like a guru
- Protects like a lioness
- Loves, guides, and even scolds when needed

Even Adhya yogi, Shiva is silent without Shakti. She is movement, fire, and life itself.

Many Faces, One Mother

Like our own mom switching between Zen master and boss mode, the Goddess wears many expressions. These aren't separate beings— they're different moods of the same divine source:

- Saraswati—The wise one: learning, music, creativity
- Lakshmi—The generous one: abundance, harmony
- Durga—The fierce one: destroys fear and injustice
- Kali—The wild protector: fierce, but guards the innocent
- Parvati—The nurturer: calm, loving, and strong in softness

Lesson?

Be smart. Be kind. Be fierce. Be loving. Just like mom.

Level Up: The Three City Supermoms

If Saraswati, Lakshmi, Durga, Kali, and Parvati are the everyday mom moods we meet at home, then Kamakshi, Meenakshi, and Vishalakshi are the power players on the big stage. Entire cities orbit around their presence, and together they form one of Hinduism's most revered goddess triads.

- Kamakshi of Kanchi (Love & Grace): The calm, seated goddess of Kanchipuram, whose gaze (kama = love) radiates compassion and union. She represents stillness, balance, and the power of love to reset the chaos button.
- Meenakshi of Madurai (Warrior Queen): The fish-eyed (meen = fish) ruler who conquered kingdoms before marrying Shiva in one of Hinduism's most famous celestial weddings. She blends political authority with divine compassion—the Devi in full boss mode.

- Vishalakshi of Kashi (Liberation & Vision): The wide-eyed (vishala = large) goddess of Varanasi, standing beside Lord Vishwanath. She embodies wisdom, infinite vision, and moksha itself. Her gaze says, "I see you, and I accept you," with no conditions attached.

The three energies are commonly referred to in one breath, and together, they represent the three powers every human need:

- Kamakshi → Heart (love and compassion)
- Meenakshi → Hands (strength and action)
- Vishalakshi → Head (wisdom and clarity)

In Shakta tradition, visiting all three is called the Shakti Triveni Yatra — a pilgrimage balancing heart, hands, and head. In modern lingo? It's the full mom-upgrade pack.

And here's the best part: you don't need a ticket to Kanchi, Madurai, or Kashi to experience Shakti. She's already with you. When you learn something new (Saraswati), share with generosity (Lakshmi), stand up for fairness (Durga), or choose calm (Parvati), you're channeling her. The same energy that sustains great cities is alive in your daily choices.

Navaratri Nights

Every year, Navaratri celebrates the Goddess in three key forms:

- Durga (strength)
- Lakshmi (abundance)
- Saraswati (wisdom)

For nine nights, we light lamps, dance, and reflect on how to bring her qualities into their lives.

Final Takeaway: Your Inner Supermom Is Divine

The Goddess isn't just a statue in a temple or a name in a book. She's the part of you that teaches, protects, comforts, and roars when needed.

- Real power isn't loud—it is loving.
- It is wise.

- It is fearless when it must be.

And the most divine thing you can be? A kind, courageous, wise human being—just like mom.

Footnote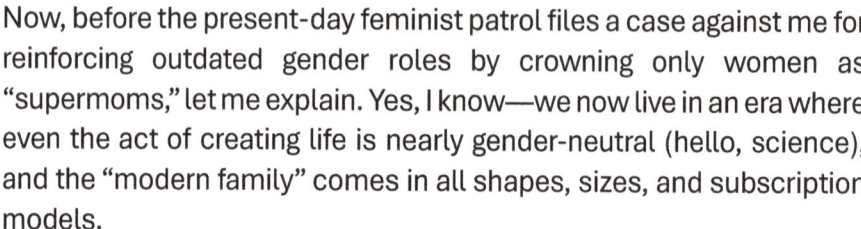

Now, before the present-day feminist patrol files a case against me for reinforcing outdated gender roles by crowning only women as "supermoms," let me explain. Yes, I know—we now live in an era where even the act of creating life is nearly gender-neutral (hello, science), and the "modern family" comes in all shapes, sizes, and subscription models.

So, attributing all child-molding duties solely to women might trigger a flurry of think pieces titled: "Why Must She Always Be the Nurturer?"

To be fair, this critique has some teeth. Unlike some baseless theories I usually dismiss with a Gandalf-style "You shall not pass," this one made me pause and think.

Because here's the truth: while the archetypal 'supermom' is symbolic, molding young minds should be a tag-team sport. Depending on the situation, any parent—regardless of gender—might find themselves donning the cape:

- Heroically negotiating the sacred snack treaty
- Packing lunchboxes like a Michelin chef for picky eaters
- Decoding toddler tantrums that defy known logic, like convincing a four-year-old princess that winter is not the time to debut her favorite pink skirt
- Mastering the bedtime routine—also known as the nightly showdown of wills

Speaking from personal experience, I had the great fortune (or karma) to play stay-at-home dad for both my kids. Thanks to a wonderfully accommodating employer who let me push my engineering job to the third shift, I got to experience full-time parenting on the frontlines.

I didn't just tolerate it — I loved it. So much so that my son, in all his eight-year-old entrepreneurial wisdom, insisted I quit engineering altogether and start "Daddy Day Care". I came dangerously close to considering it, too. Spoiler alert — I eventually did start something along those lines. But that's a story for another book.

The takeaway? Dads, it is time to unlock your inner supermom. Because true equality isn't just about who earns more or who changes the occasional diaper—it is about showing up, day in and day out, with all the love, energy, and snack-planning genius traditionally associated with moms.

Equal parenting means equal opportunity to be covered in glitter, yogurt, and existential dread—sometimes all before 9 a.m.

Field Guide: Chapter 4—The Goddess: Your Inner Supermom

WHO IS THE GODDESS?

- Shakti = Power. The energy behind everything in the universe.
- She is the life force, love, protection, and nurturing.
- First form of Shakti you meet = your mother.
- Even Shiva is silent without her—she is movement, fire, life.

HER MANY FACES (JUST LIKE YOUR MOM!)

- Saraswati—Teaches and guides with wisdom.
- Lakshmi—Feeds, manages, and provides.
- Durga—Protects and stands strong.
- Kali—Gets fierce when justice is needed.
- Parvati—The calm, loving, gentle side.

SHINE WITH SHAKTI

- Learn with Saraswati energy.
- Share with Lakshmi's heart.
- Stand up with Durga's courage.
- Show patience like Parvati's grace.

NAVARATRI NIGHTS

- Nine nights of celebrating Durga, Lakshmi, Saraswati.
- Also, nine chances to honor your mom—the goddess at home.

QUOTE TO REMEMBER

'Your first temple was your home, and your first goddess was your mother'.

Section 2:

🧭 Spiritual Wi-Fi Zones —Roaming from Bharat to Kerala

CHAPTER 5
HOLY VIBES, DIFFERENT TRIBES
NORTH-SOUTH EDITION

Chapter 5: Holy Vibes, Different Tribes — North–South Edition

Now that we have explored what Hinduism is at its core—the big ideas, cosmic cycles, and the whole divine download of dharma—it is time to zoom in a little closer. Because here's the twist: Hinduism isn't a one-size-fits-all kind of religion. It shapeshifts across landscapes, languages, and even lunch menus. In this chapter, we will see how the same Sanatana Dharma wears different clothes in different places—especially in the great cultural tug-of-war (and mutual admiration society) between the North and the South.

So, you walk into a temple in Delhi, then one in Thiruvananthapuram, and you're like— "Wait, is this even the same religion?"

Short answer? Yes.

Longer answer? Welcome to Sanatana Dharma—a spiritual multiverse where different outfits, chants, snacks, and rituals still connect to the same divine Wi-Fi.

Think of it as the same spiritual playlist, remixed in two very different regional styles—it is more like a spiritual buffet.

Same Roots, Spicy Branches

Hinduism is like a banyan tree. Its roots? Ancient—Vedas, dharma, karma, moksha. Its branches? Wild and varied—bhajans in Bhojpuri here, Tamil chants there, all part of the same sacred ecosystem.

Same core beliefs, different regional seasoning. In North India, it is gulal (red powder) in the air and Ram Leela in full swing. Down South, you have oil baths, jasmine braids, and temple towers that look like rainbow-layered wedding cakes. Same gods, same Vedas—but the vibe? Totally different.

Temples: The Sacred Architecture Wars

North India:

- Temples with beehive-style shikharas, stretching up as if they are trying to reach 5G divinity.
- Bhajans, bells, and dramatic darshan moments bring the divine into daily life.

South India:

- Gopurams stacked like god-level Jenga towers—each floor covered in deity drama.
- Agama-based rituals choreographed with precision—every bell, flower, and incense puff have a purpose.

Bonus Dress Code Drama:

- South: Mundus preferred, shirts optional—sacred minimalism.
- North: "Come as you are," but maybe skip the ripped jeans in temples.

Festival Feels: One Holiday, Infinite Versions

Diwali:

- North: Fireworks, Lakshmi Pooja, sweets, and glitter chaos.
- South: Oil baths at dawn, new clothes, and Krishna dunking on Narakasura.

Navaratri:

- South: Golu doll displays, devotional singing, and snack diplomacy.
- North: Ramlila plays, Ravana fireworks, and full-on dramatic dharma replays.

Regionals:

- Onam (Kerala): Pookalam, sadyas, boat races, and Mahabali nostalgia.
- Pongal (Tamil Nadu): Sugarcane, sun worship, and sacred cow love.

- Holi: Full-throttle color riot in the North; subtle, flower-powered version in the South.

Language and Music: Your Spiritual Soundtrack

Sanskrit might be the blueprint, but the vibes get local fast.

South India:

- Tamil, Malayalam, Telugu, Kannada—each with bhakti poetry that slaps.
- Alwars and Nayanars = Bhakti influencers before it was cool.
- Carnatic music: Focused, structured, temple-mode with technical fire.

North India:

- Hindi, Braj, Bhojpuri = Home of heart-tugging bhajans 🧡.
- Hindustani music: Soulful, free-forming, meditative with creative flair.

Same Gods, New Drip

Shiva's still Shiva—but in Kedarnath, he's the mountain yogi, in Chidambaram, he's Nataraja in cosmic dance mode. Vishnu's look shifts from minimalist to maximalist depending on the region.

Hinduism doesn't just allow these remix versions—it celebrates them. The divine stays constant, but the outfit changes depending on the postcode.

Final Download: One Dharma, Many Dialects

Whether you're lighting lamps to a nadaswaram in a Kerala temple or humming bhajans with harmonium backup in Mathura, you're still plugged into the same cosmic mainframe. Same soul, different swag.

Team Dharma, for the win.

Field Guide: Holy Vibes, Different Tribes – North-South Edition

Temples: 🛕 North: Beehive-style shikharas | South: Gopuram towers like rainbow wedding cakes

Dress Code: 👕 North: Casual, just no ripped jeans | 🧎 South: Mundus and sacred minimalism

Diwali: 🪔 North: Fireworks & Lakshmi Puja | 🛁 South: Oil baths & Narakasura story

Navaratri: 🪔 South: Golu dolls & Ayudha Puja | 🎭 North: Ramlila plays & Ravana effigies

Regional Festivals: 🌼 Onam | 🌞 Pongal | 🎨 Holi (Color riot vs. flower gentle)

Music & Language: 🎶 Carnatic (South) – fast, temple mode | 🎵 Hindustani (North) – meditative raga

Gods' Avatars: 🕉️ Shiva: Yogi in Kedarnath, Dancer in Chidambaram | Vishnu: From simple to majestic

Spiritual Wi-Fi: 📶 All paths lead to the same divine signal—just different regional routers

INTERLUDE 1: WHATSAPP WARS: THE NORTH–SOUTH SAGA–A PATRIOTIC RANT WITH POPCORN AND DHARMA

So, one of my college WhatsApp groups has recently turned into something between The Avengers: Civil War and Kung Fu Panda 4: Rise of the Regional Languages. One side is passionately arguing that the South is basically a separate country—no Hindi, thank you very much; we already survived one colonial language, and English at least comes with LinkedIn benefits.

The other side is like, "Relax, no one's enforcing the Goblet of Fire. It's just Hindi as a third language, not a magical binding contract."

Here's the thing: Whether these arguments are political, poetic, or just peak procrastination, we're missing the big picture faster than Ron missed the Horcrux in the locket.

You might wear mundus in the South and sherwanis in the North, but guess what? The yajna fire burns in both, the mantras still echo "?," and they both bow to something beyond.

I try not to get pulled into these debates and that's not out of confusion—I stay out because "my vision of Bharat is not pixelated". It's whole, sacred, and gloriously diverse. I see Bharat not as fragments of culture in competition, but as different Avengers in the same multiverse. And Hinduism? It's the ancient script running all the timelines, not some linguistic update patch.

Let us not split dharma down language lines. Because if Thor can hang with Korg without speaking Asgardian, then we can definitely learn one more language without combusting our cultural circuits.

So yeah—keep your Malayalam, love your Tamil, develop around Kannada, celebrate Telugu pride, and let Mumbai be the melting pot it always was. But remember, before we were South or North, we were all Sanatanis 🕉️.

Chapter 6:

How Kerala Became Kerala –

A COOL TIME-TRAVEL ADVENTURE

Chapter 6: How Kerala Became Kerala—A Cool Time-Travel Adventure

So now that you've got your all-India upgrade—Dharma decoded, chakras aligned, and maybe even a spiritual glow-up worthy of Doctor Strange's approval, it is time to swipe right on one specific state: Kerala. If India is Hogwarts, Kerala is that secret Room of Requirement full of coconut oil, temple drums, and ancestral Wi-Fi. Think of it as the Avenger who's not loud but always clutch, like Ant-Man with ancient rituals. It is Po's Valley of Peace with monsoon mode activated. And yes, it is also the Bikini Bottom of Indian culture: a little weird, super deep, and always unexpectedly wise. Ready? Let's dive into the land where even the rain seems to know Sanskrit. Long before backwaters and banana chips, Kerala's story began over 3000 years ago—with rainforests, spice ships, and sacred groves.

And how exactly did this little strip of land between the Arabian Sea and the Western Ghats become one of the most culturally vibrant corners of India?

Let us hop on our imaginary time machine (or maybe the Time-Turner, or Doctor Strange's Sling Ring) and zoom through the first thousand years of Kerala's past—no passport or visa required (if you are in Bharat legally!)

Part I: Pre-1000 BCE—Forest Life and Early Trade

Once Upon a Time in the Jungle...

Before Insta reels and resort life, Kerala was all rivers, forests, and mystery. Life here was pretty primal — think cave chic meets barefoot explorer.

- Mega rivers like Periyar and Pampa
- Rains that didn't ask permission before pouring

A green explosion of forests, animals, and herbal secrets

Kerala's First Influencers—The Tribal Geniuses

The earliest people to live here were tribal communities like the Paniyas, Kurumbas, and Kattunaikkans. No social media, but they really knew how to vibe with nature. More Shifu than influencer:

- Forest spirits
- Sacred animals
- Super chill groves called Kaavu (sacred forest shrines where rituals still happen today)

Their legacy still lives on through dramatic rituals like Theyyam. Basically, they nailed eco-friendly living before it was trendy.

Enter the Spice Hype

Even way back in 1000 BCE, Kerala was famous for spices — especially for black pepper!

- Traders from Egypt, Mesopotamia, and Phoenicia came sailing in
- Muziris (near modern Kodungallur) became the hottest hangout

Pepper was literally worth its weight in gold

The Chera Kings and The Tamil Connection

By around 300 BCE, Kerala was part of Tamilakam, a region with major poetic swagger—we are talking Sangam Era vibes.

- The Chera dynasty ruled the roost
- Kings like Uthiyan Cheralathan were part-time warriors, full-time patrons of art
- Sangam poems mention their generosity and valor

Worship, the OG Way

Before fancy temples and rituals, Kerala's people worshipped:

- Snakes
- The Mother Goddess
- Ancestors
- Nature

Later, Buddhism, Jainism, and Vedic Hinduism added more layers—but the original flavor stayed local and sacred.

Part II: 0 to 1000 CE—From Spice Ports to Temple Culture

Port Cities and Ancient Swag

Kerala became the place to be. Here's why:

- Roman coins and wine jars (amphorae) turned up in digs
- Muziris got a shout-out in a Greek travel guide
- Traders brought silk, gold, and perfumes—locals gave them spices and a warm welcome

Kerala, Spiritual Melting Pot Edition

Faiths flowed in like the monsoon:

- Christianity may have arrived in 52 CE via St. Thomas
- Jewish communities appeared after 70 CE
- Buddhism and Jainism dominated for centuries
- Vedic Hinduism blended in later like ghee on hot rice

Hello, Islam — Peacefully, please. No conversions, live and let live!!

By the 7th century, Arab traders brought more than goods:

- The Cheraman Juma Masjid (built in ~700 CE) is India's first mosque
- Muslim settlers were welcomed by local rulers
- The Mappila (Tamil word for son-in-law) Muslim community blended tradition with trade

The Cheras Strike Back

By 800 CE, the Chera kings returned for a sequel—and it was a hit (Avengers-style):

- New capital: Mahodayapuram (a.k.a. Kodungallur)
- King Kulasekhara Alvar went full Bhakti mode
- Copper plate inscriptions became receipts of the past

Temples = Culture + Curry Leaves

With the arrival of Brahmin communities (Namboothiris):

- Scholarly villages called Agraharams popped up
- Temples became schools, theaters, and spiritual Google Search centers
- Art forms like Koodiyattam and early Kathakali were born

Malayalam Enters the Chat

By the 9th century:

- Malayalam began to step out from Tamil's shadow
- Copper plates like Tharisapalli Cheppedu showed early writing
- Sanskrit became Malayalam's fancy BFF

Final Thought: Kerala, Where Everyone's Invited

Kerala didn't grow by isolating itself. It grew by welcoming people, ideas, faiths, and flavors—then blending them into something totally its own.

So next time someone asks why Kerala's so unique, tell them it is because this land has always been:

- A cultural mash-up
- A spiritual buffet
- And a living, breathing time capsule

From sacred groves to spice ports, Kerala didn't just preserve its roots—it let new routes take root too.

And the remix continues…

Field Guide: Chapter 6 – How Kerala Became Kerala

TIMELINE SNAPSHOT

- 🏛 1000 BCE – Black pepper trade begins; Kerala enters the ancient global economy.
- 🏛 300 BCE – Chera dynasty joins the Sangam scene.
- ✝ 52 CE – St. Thomas brings Christianity to Kerala.
- 🕌 700 CE – Cheraman Juma Masjid is built.
- 🛕 800 CE – Bhakti-era Cheras rise again.
- 🗣 900 CE – Malayalam begins standing on its own linguistic feet.

CULTURE HACKS FROM HISTORY

- 🌳 Kaavu – Sacred groves = Ancient eco-temples.
- 💃 Theyyam – Tribal ritual theatre that survived into pop culture.
- 🎉 Temple Utsavams – Spiritual meets spectacle meets street food.

TRADE TRIVIA

- ⚖ Pepper was worth its weight in gold. Literally.
- 🍷 Muziris had Roman wine before Goa had feni.
- 🏺 Amphorae = Ancient Tupperware for elite spice deals.

SPIRITUAL DOWNLOAD

- 🕊 Kerala = Not just Hindu. Also, Buddhist, Jain, Christian, Jewish, and Muslim — all living their best interfaith lives.
- 🏛 Temples were once classrooms, theatres, and councils, not just prayer zones.

QUOTE TO REMEMBER

🌀 "Kerala's story is a remix of roots and routes—and it's still being written."

CHAPTER 7: CASTE AND CURIOUS —GODS MUST BE CRAZY

Caste, Class, and Chaos: A Crash Course in Varna, Jati, and All That Jazz

(Recommended reading: Varna, Jati, Caste: A Primer on Indian Social Structures—Rajiv Malhotra and Vijaya Viswanathan)

We have wandered through Kerala's rain-drenched jungles, dined with ancient traders, and vibed with gods in sacred groves; basically, a full-on historical binge-watch. But here's the plot twist: beneath all that cultural brilliance, something else was simmering. Like realizing the Avengers HQ has an HR problem no one talks about.

Caste wasn't just a background detail—it shaped who got to chant mantras, who got to serve the rice, and who got to sit where. Even Po had to face the "you're just a noodle guy" moment before becoming the Dragon Warrior. Before we go back to dancing with Theyyam and making temple runs, we need to zoom in on this layered, loaded social code that's shaped Hindu society—and take a look at how it played out across India… and eventually, in Kerala.

Indian society's social setup? More complicated than your group chat drama. So, here's your cheat sheet:

- Varna: ancient job-based Hogwarts houses
- Brahmins: spiritual nerds
- Kshatriyas: warrior kings
- Vaishyas: side-hustling traders

Shudras: the get-it-done crew

Originally based on skills and profession, not birth. In theory, you could level up or switch tracks—like switching from Slytherin to Gryffindor. But theory rarely survives power politics.

- Jati = neighborhood cliques, but with thousands of versions and their own dosas.

- Caste system = when this whole vibe turned into a no-exit birth certificate.

Then came the British, who added spreadsheets and nasal measurements, and voilà: chaos became caste-coded forever.

How Brahmins Became the Narrative MVPs (and Lost the Plot) 📜

Here's how the Brahmins went from helpful priests to spiritual gatekeepers:

- 1500 BCE: Indo-Aryans arrive. Fire rituals go mainstream
- 1000 BCE: Only Brahmins can chant. Everyone else just listens
- 600 BCE: Buddha and Mahavira start the 'caste? No thanks' club
- 200 BCE–300 CE: Epics drop. Brahmins become narrative MVPs
- 300–800 CE: Manusmriti drops like an iOS update. Caste = law
- 800–1200 CE: Brahmin VIP clubs a.k.a. temples, become invite-only

How Bad Did It Get?

Like K-drama bad. Society.exe had officially crashed—and no one was rebooting:

- Untouchability: Your shadow was offensive
- Temple rules: Show your Sanskrit credentials or leave
- Culture: Only upper castes could perform sacred arts
- Women: Either locked away or exploited, depending on your caste

The Reboot: Ambedkar and The Rise of 'Nope'

Time for a software update:

- Ambedkar drafted the Constitution and hit CTRL+Z on caste injustice
- Temple entry reform challenged the gatekeeping
- Education broke the Sanskrit monopoly
- Culture rebooted with Dalit art, music, and voices
- Social media = today's protest tool. Reels, threads, and savage clapbacks against casteism.

Your caste? No longer your karma. Just part of history's deleted files

How the British Made It Worse

Because obviously, colonialism wasn't content with stealing spices:

- Caste census (1872–1931): People were forced to pick a caste—some for the first time ever
- Herbert Risley's Nose Index: Yes, a British official measured noses to determine race and caste. (Yikes.)
- Manusmriti revival: Colonial courts loved it. Ancient patriarchy + British bureaucracy = nightmare collab
- Job = caste = forever: Records ensured your ancestor's job became your job title. Permanently

Final Word: Mic Drop. Mundu Swipe. Exit Stage Left

Questioning mythology. Calling out injustice. Reforming culture.

This legacy lives in:

- Every student who questions
- Every poet who protests
- Every meme that calls out inequality

If society's system still glitches? You know the command:

Breaking the Bounds of Holy Inequality

Wait, Aren't Other Religions Better?

Indian Christians and Muslims—many of whom were once Hindus—often criticized caste as if they had escaped its gravity.

But here's the twist: Islam and Christianity? Also, not exactly caste-free utopias:

- Christianity: Caste-like discrimination exists among Dalit Christians. Even globally, Sunday is often still 'the most segregated day of the week'

- Islam: Preaches equality, but biradari systems and Sayyid privilege exist in many Muslim societies. And let's not even start on women's rights in Islam—they are virtually non-existent.

Spoiler: Hierarchy is a Human Bug, Not a Hindu One

Turns out, the urge to create hierarchies and draw lines between 'us' and 'them' isn't a Hindu glitch.

It's a full-blown human feature.

Religions don't invent inequality. People do. And they bring that baggage into every faith they enter—sometimes with hashtags #notblessed.

Kabhi Privilege Kabhi Oppression: Divine Disparity Drama

And while this was the scene across India, Kerala's version of the caste story? Well… it came with sandalwood oil, steel umbrellas, and a lot more fire. Flip the page.

Mini Myth Buster: SB 403—What's the Real Deal?

Those of you in the USA may have heard the recent controversy around California's SB 403—a bill that claimed to fight caste discrimination but ended up putting Hindu Americans under a suspicious spotlight. What looked like justice on paper turned into a subtle stereotype grenade. Let's break it down, minus the drama, and with all the receipts.

Myth

"SB 403 was just about banning caste. Why would Hindus even oppose it?"

Truth Drop

Because it wasn't neutral—it was Hindu-coded. While caste discrimination is wrong, SB 403 painted Hinduism as the root of it all, ignoring that caste exists across religions.

Who Started It?

California Senator Aisha Wahab (a Muslim) introduced the bill in 2023, saying it aimed to protect Dalits and others from caste bias in the US.

What It Did:

- Tried to add "caste" as a new category in California law
- Repeatedly spotlighted Hindus
- Ignored existing protections already in place

Why It Hurt:

- Made Hindu kids feel like they're wearing a target
- Ignored caste issues in other communities
- Turned a fight for justice into a culture blame game

Who Fought Back?

Groups like CoHNA (Coalition of Hindus of North America) and the Hindu American Foundation (HAF) stepped up big time. From community mobilization and Capitol rallies to legal memos and media rebuttals, these organizations worked tirelessly to explain why the bill, while well-intentioned, risked turning Hindu Americans into scapegoats. Their advocacy played a key role in Governor Newsom's decision to veto the bill.

You can fight injustice without shaming your culture.

Pride ≠ prejudice.

Be the generation that fixes things with facts, not fear.

What Every Hindu American Should Know:

Soft anti-Hindu narratives like SB 403 aren't rare glitches—they are recurring bugs in the system. They may not burn flags, but they quietly chip away at identity. It's up to us to be aware, equipped, and unapologetically informed. Know your roots. Understand caste with context. And always remember: caste isn't exclusive to Hinduism; it's a social problem across faiths. Truth is your best defense.

Chapter 8: Kerala's Social Ladder—Slippery, Oily, and Historically Hostile

Opener: "From Mic Drops to Mana Drops — Enter Kerala's Endgame"

While Chapter 7 gave you the all-India chaos—with Brahmins scripting their own BCU timeline, Buddha playing the rebel Jedi, and Ambedkar pressing CTRL+Z on 2,000 years of glitches—Kerala was quietly brewing its own plot twist. Spicier. Oilier. Trickier.

Here's the twist: caste in Kerala wasn't just a ladder. It was a slippery, oil-coated stepladder with lasers, caste-coded shadows, and GPS-level purity zones. You didn't just get ranked by birth—you got assigned proximity privileges, like Hogwarts spells that only worked if you were *this pure or richer*. Even shadows weren't safe. Yes, your literal shadow could be too low caste to exist. Welcome to the original Social Distancing Simulator: 1500 BCE edition.

🕉 vs 🕉 - Namboothiris vs Iyers: The OG Brahmin Showdown—Kerala Edition

We have two distinct types of Brahmins in Kerala—the namboohthiri and the Iyer (a.k.a. pattar). Imagine two ancient squads rolling into Kerala like rival superhero teams—but instead of capes and laser eyes, they came with mantras, rituals, and some serious Sanskrit swag.

Team Namboothiri: The "Srautha Supremes"

These were the Doctor Stranges of Kerala — Vedic masters who worshipped Agni (fire god) like it was their BFF. They performed yagnas (think magical fire-based rituals, no goats harmed) and followed Srautha tantra, which is basically the OG Vedic code of conduct—powered by "shruti" (sacred sounds).

Legend says they traveled through a portal into Kerala from the Gangetic plains or maybe Andhra, Sanskrit scrolls in tow. They dropped Sanskrit like Thor drops his hammer—with epic impact—and it blended with local Tamil to cook up Malayalam, our homegrown language.

And oh, these guys weren't just priesting around—they made money moves. They impressed the local kings (a.k.a. the Nair chieftains) and became mega landlords. Like actual Zamindar-level real estate bosses, living in sprawling manas and illams (fancy ancestral homes) with nalu (4) kettus (rooms), ettu (8) kettus, and even 24-room palaces. Why? Because they followed the primogeniture system— only the eldest bro got the loot, so the mansion didn't get chopped up like a birthday cake.

Team Iyer: The "Mantra Masters"

Now enter the Iyers—Tamil Nadu's spiritual squad—the Kung Fu Pandas of daily deity devotion. These folks weren't about fire rituals but loved chanting mantras and doing peaceful poojas to their fav gods like Shiva, Vishnu, Ganesha... you name it.

When they came to Kerala, the temple gates were already Namboothiri-only zones. So, the Iyers got shuffled to support roles; not priests but still doing important behind-the-scenes temple work. Think of them like the IT crew at Hogwarts. Not always center stage but keeping the magic flowing.

Economically, though, it was kind of like Tony Stark vs. Peter Parker. While the Namboothiris were living large in manas and illams (mansions), Iyers lived in humble agraharams—tight row houses near temples, with just one door at the front and one at the back. No windows = no peeking.

Impact Summary:

Kerala's caste remix didn't just break the system—it made a new one. One where:

- The Namboothiris built Sanskrit-fortified mansions (with strict inheritance rules).
- The Iyers built faith-filled row houses just outside the temple spotlight.
- And everyone else? Pushed out of the frame like background extras in a show they helped build.

Extreme Social Distancing, Ancient Edition

Caste in Kerala wasn't just about birth. It was about space—literal, physical space 🫸. Touching a 'higher' caste person was considered polluting. But Kerala didn't stop there. Just walking near an upper-caste person or being seen by them was prohibited and had serious consequences.

If you were Pulayar, you had to shout out and clear the road—or risk death just for being visible. Temples, schools, and even shared breezes were off-limits. Social distancing level: 100. Like Hogwarts House Elves, but way less magical and far more tragic.

Even Christians Got Caste-ified

Even Syrian Christians, technically outside the Hindu caste system, followed the same caste rules. Touch a 'lower' caste person? Take a bath. Yeah—Jesus probably wouldn't have approved. This wasn't 'turn the other cheek,' this was 'go scrub off the vibes.' And just when you thought it couldn't get any more layered...

500 Shades of Division

By the 1800s, Kerala had built the most extreme, complicated caste structure in India. Over 500 caste groups, each with a designated rank on a ladder where even your shadow could be too low to matter. Lower caste communities were pushed out of village centers and into the periphery—literally and socially. Basically, if Kerala society were a Marvel lineup, half the heroes were never even called into the plot.

Resistance and Reform

Then came reformers. The Constitution in 1947 banned caste discrimination—but mindsets don't vanish with a signature. Many still carry caste baggage—sometimes subtly, sometimes not. Like that Hogwarts student still clinging to their house points from year one.

The Rebel in a Mundu: V.T. Bhattathiripad

While most were busy chanting slokas, Bhattathiripad (himself an orthodox Brahmin) rolled up and asked, "Wait, why are we using mythology to justify oppression?" He called out the 'Gods' and rewired the epics—with logic, sass, and fearless reform.

Logic Wins

Let's break it down like Netflix seasons:

- Season 1: Dashavatara—Evolution or Just Brahmin Fan Fiction?

  Vishnu's 10 avatars = divine Pokémon evolution. But Bhattathiripad would ask, "Where's the Shudra DLC?"

- Season 2: Mahabharata—Moral Lessons with Major Side-Eye

  Draupadi's disrobing receives lectures instead of justice. Bhattathiripad probably facepalmed hard.

- Season 3: Ramayana—Communication Issues in a Chariot

  Rama builds a bridge to Lanka, but can't build emotional bridges with Sita? Bhattathiripad: "Trial by fire? More like fragile male ego."

  He didn't burn books—he rewrote them, despite facing social backlash and isolation.

Still Climbing the Ladder

But here's the thing—Kerala didn't just retire its old ladder of hierarchies. It swapped them out for new ones, dressed up in modern language like "secularism" and "equality." Different script, same imbalance.

The Constitution may have banned caste, but Kerala didn't exactly become a social utopia overnight. Old hierarchies didn't vanish, they just shape shifted.

Take "Kerala-style secularism." In theory, it was about fairness. In practice, it often meant Hindu temples like Guruvayur and Sabarimala were taken over by the state; churches and mosques remained firmly in community hands. Add in vote-bank politics, minority quotas, and reservation policies that sometimes favored the already privileged, and you get a new kind of imbalance: a majority community carrying the weight of "neutrality."

Cue the Sabarimala storm: a centuries-old vow of celibate devotion was reframed as "anti-women" by courts and activists who hadn't even opened the glossary on naishthika brahmacharya. The fallout? Protests, polarization, and yet another example of how Kerala's ladder of inclusion keeps getting rebuilt—with different labels, same imbalance.

Today's Struggle

The Constitution gives reservations and rights to Scheduled Castes and Tribes to help level the playing field. The worst of caste is in the past, but the struggle for true equality is real. Kerala wasn't just a system, it was a full-blown manual on dividing people by birth, space, and now, sometimes, by law.

Until we hit Ctrl+Z on imaginary caste lines and trade ego shields for inclusion cloaks, we'll stay stuck in a chaotic time-loop, one Lokiverse short of collapse.

This isn't shade aimed at the few selfless heroes already fighting the good fight. Respect. But imagine how much more we could do if we dropped the elitist filters and chose dignity over division.

Because in the end, the real dharma flex isn't how many rituals you fund but how many people you uplift while doing it.

🎁 Bonus Scroll: Kerala Hindus 3.0 — Marx, Mantras, and Multiverse Madness

In the land of modern Kerala Hindus, we have done what even the Avengers couldn't: become pro-revolution, pro-tradition, and pro-whatever's trending on Instagram, all at the same time.

The Diaspora Multiverse of Madness

We chant the Gayatri mantra while binge-watching Sacred Games, host Satyanarayana poojas, then dive into the next RSS vs. CPM Facebook war like it's a Quidditch final.

But hey, that's the beauty of Kerala Hinduism 3.0 — a glorious mess of pickled contradictions. And after all the hartals and revolutionary spells, we migrated: from Kerala — to the Gulf, the UK, the US, Down Under, and the joke is that there could be a Malayali-run tea stall even on the South Side of The Moon!!

We sorted ourselves with more efficiency than Hogwarts' Sorting Hat. Diaspora 3.0 just upgraded the tech: Google Forms, Zoom calls, IRS-approved 501(c)(3) status.

Now imagine all those contradictions — but in Queens, Melbourne, London, or Dubai.

Welcome to the Kerala Hindu diaspora multiverse, where every second building is either a strip mall or a temple funded by three rival Ayyappa groups and four flavors of Nair samajams.

We may not always make sense. But we always make a scene. And we do it all with coconut oil, confusion, and unmatched charisma.

📣 A Message to the next generation: Claim the Code, Don't Just Copy It

> Let's be real — these organizations mean well. They've kept the spirit running in strip malls, printed souvenir magazines with 47 sponsor logos, and somehow managed to feed 400 people hot sadhya twice every year. But when it comes to firing up the youth? Nada. Zip. Still buffering!! There's still **serious*• room for a glow-up.

Is it enough to do an Onam group dance or kaikottikali once a year and call it heritage? And there are these grand conventions — where the focus has largely shifted to grand banquets, parading in designer attire, Insta-worthy backdrops, and collecting Facebook friend requests from people you may never meet again, all while pretending it's about culture and the next generation.

Now, dear young reader, it's *your* turn — not just to participate, but to lead, reform, reshape, and reinvent.

Because one day, it won't be you awkwardly explaining why we don't eat meat on certain days or pull an all-nighter (Shivaratri) randomly — it'll be your kids. And don't you want them to feel proud, not pressured? Confident, not confused? To know that their Sanatani roots aren't something to "tone down" around their western friends, but something to flex?

So, show up. Run for office. Rewrite the bylaws. Start the podcast. Host the Satsang with a more rewarding agenda (but keep the snacks). Do fewer but more meaningful conventions and showy events. Break down those caste boundaries and unite these organizations as "one Hindu organization". Infuse these spaces with your fire, your memes, your playlists, your clarity. Because the future of our cultural pride won't be saved by nostalgia — it will be saved by *you*.

Moral of the story?

If Kerala is a country, it's got SpongeBob's logic, Thanos' sense of balance, Po's clumsiness, and Harry Potter's identity crisis. And you, dear reader, are the chosen one—tasked with laughing at it, loving it, and fixing it.

Good luck. You are going to need a prasadam power-up.

Section 3:

🛕 Sacred Geometry, Everyday Energy

Chapter 9:

THE HINDU TEMPLE—

MORE THAN JUST A FANCY BUILDING WITH BELLS

CHAPTER 9: THE HINDU TEMPLE —MORE THAN JUST A FANCY BUILDING WITH BELLS

So... have you ever stepped into a Hindu temple and suddenly felt a weird buzz—like your brain just entered Zen Mode? That calm? That tingle? That "Whoa, something serious is going on here" vibe?

⚠️ **Spoiler alert: It's not just your imagination—or leftover sugar from the prasadam.**

Hindu temples aren't just pretty buildings with bells, lamps, and long lines. Nope. They are power spots—carefully designed with math, mantras, and mega vibes to help you feel balanced, grounded, and maybe even a little cosmic.

We are talking architecture aligned with Earth's magnetic fields, acoustic engineering that amplifies chanting, and layouts that guide your mind from chaos to calm—faster than your meditation app.

📌 **Place of Prayer vs. Place of Worship**

But before we go full "temple explorer," let's clear up one major thing:

Not all places where people pray are the same.

Some are just places of prayer—a quick spiritual pit-stop where you whisper some lines, maybe toss in a wish, and bounce. Kinda like sending a text to the divine... with no read receipts.

Take, for instance, how some Muslims roll out their prayer mats on highways, footpaths, or literally wherever they feel the Mecca-connection urge. It's like a sacred flash mob—mostly orderly and organized, direction-locked, and zero concern for traffic or the rickshaw guy just trying to get home.

But a place of worship? Now that's a whole different beast. Or should we say... a whole different Master Shifu-level energy portal.

Hindu temples aren't just "assigned spiritual corners." They are built with surgical precision — like if Hogwarts had a baby with NASA and taught it Vedic physics.

You can't just drop a temple anywhere and expect the spiritual Wi-Fi to work. The blueprint is cosmic.

- Location based on planetary energy zones
- Architecture aligned with magnetic fields
- Acoustics tuned for mantra amplification

🪔 Metal alloys engineered to capture and transmit vibrations

And mantra recitations (mantra-uchcharana) that literally reset your brain's chakra software.

TL; DR: It's not just a building. It's a vibe machine.

📦 Bonus Round: Temples in the Wild (a.k.a. Strip Mall Sanctums)

Unless, of course, you're in the USA—where your brand-new temple might've been a toy store last month and a discount sofa warehouse the month before.

Welcome to Strip Mall Sanctum™, where Lord Ganesha now blesses you from behind what used to be Aisle 3 of "ABC Furniture & Co."

But hey, no judgment. When you can't align with magnetic fields, you align with lease agreements.

That's when our desi Doctor Stranges pull out the real magic—some astro-remedies, a dash of Vastu wizardry, and enough incense to confuse a smoke detector.

The goal? To convert that spiritually suspicious real estate into at least a 5G-level cosmic hotspot. Not quite Kailasa, but good enough for a proper mantra upgrade and soul reboot—basically the Wi-Fi equivalent of Po doing inner peace in a food court.

And while on Temples, guess what?

Kerala is basically the Wakanda of temple energy—hidden in plain sight, glowing with ancient tech, and blessed with next-level spiritual vibes.

We are talking about legendary, soul-recharging sanctuaries where even Po would drop his dumplings and strike a full lotus pose.

These temples have backstories deeper than the Room of Requirement, secrets worthy of a Hogwarts restricted section, and more plot twists than a Marvel post-credit scene.

Some hide underground tunnels (basically Indiana Jones meets Kerala vibes), some feature musical pillars (no Bluetooth required), and some house deities you literally can't look at—because even gods enjoy a little low-key Invisibility Cloak now and then.

So, grab your flower offering and get ready to temple-hop across Kerala.

Not just to gawk at the architecture—but to decode the science, soul, and sparkle baked into every sacred square inch.

Let us find out what makes these temples more than bricks and bells—and why your ancestors built them with more accuracy than Tony Stark in a cave with a box of scraps.

- **Padmanabhaswamy Temple— "The Anantha Shayana Posture"**

📍 Thiruvananthapuram, Kerala

🛏️ Vishnu in Anantha Shayana (cosmic sleep mode)

🔥 Why It's Cool:

💰 One of the richest temples ever. Vishnu lounges on a five-headed serpent guarding secrets and treasure.

🕉️ Ritual Radar:

👕 Traditional attire only

🔱 See Vishnu in three parts: head, body, and feet through three doors.

⚡ Power Meter: 10/10—Old money + deep vibes = top-tier dharma credit

💡 Hot Tip: 🕉️ Visit during Murajapam or Alpashy for a full-on chanting experience.

- **Sabarimala— "The Trek to Transcendence"**

📍 Periyar Tiger Reserve, Kerala

🧘 Lord Ayyappa, yogi-warrior hybrid

🔥 Why It's Cool:

🥾 Massive yearly pilgrimage. 41 days of preparation + forest trek = spiritual XP overload.

🕉️ Ritual Radar:

🌀 Mandala Vratham fasting

🎒 Irumudi kettu (sacred gear) required

⚡ Power Meter: 11/10—Bhakti + trekking = unlocked god mode

💡 Hot Tip: 🌲 The journey is the temple. Treat the forest like your ashram.

- **Chottanikkara Temple— "Goddess on Call"**

📍 Near Ernakulam, Kerala

👑 Bhagavati as Saraswati (a.m.), Lakshmi (Noon), Durga (p.m.)

🔥 Why It's Cool:

🌀 Renowned for healing and energy clearing. Triple goddess = triple strength.

🕉️ Ritual Radar:

🌄 Goddess changes form 3x a day

🩸 Guruthi Pooja on Tuesdays = high-energy cleanse

⚡ Power Meter: 9/10—Triple boost from divine energy modes

💡 Hot Tip: ♻️ Don't miss the daily transformation. A divine transformer with healing powers.

- **Ambalapuzha Temple— "Payasam Palace"**

📍 Alappuzha, Kerala

👶 Krishna as Unnikannan (little prankster god)

🔥 Why It's Cool:

🍚 Legendary paal payasam since the 15th century = sacred dessert goals.

🕉️ Ritual Radar:

🛕 No idol during Utsavam—it's out visiting

🍲 Midday offering = the main event

⚡ Power Meter: 8.5/10—Child-god charm + payasam magic

💡 Hot Tip: ⏰ Go early if you want that holy pudding. It's divine and in demand.

- **Kadampuzha Temple— "Goddess Without an Idol"**

📍 Malappuram, Kerala

🔥 Durga as Chandi, in a formless pit of fire

🔥 Why It's Cool:

🖋 The goddess isn't visible. She's symbolized by a sacred fire pit. Powerful rituals, zero idols.

🕉 Ritual Radar:

🔮 Muttarukkal ritual for removing obstacles

🪔 Poomoodal (shower of flowers) to invoke blessings

⚡ Power Meter: 9.5/10—Invisible energy, visible impact

💡 Hot Tip: 🌼 Book pooja slots early—it gets packed during special days like Tuesdays and Fridays.

- **Guruvayoor Temple— "Vishnu's HQ"**

📍 Guruvayoor, Thrissur, Kerala

🎻 Krishna as Guruvayoorappan, a full-blown Vishnu avatar

🔥 Why It's Cool:

🛕 Most visited Krishna shrine in Kerala, called 'Bhooloka Vaikuntha' (Heaven on Earth).

🕉️ Ritual Radar:

🧘 Early morning darshan rush

🎶 Melam, elephant processions, and chembai music vibes

🚩 Power Meter: 10/10—Bhakti central with devotional traffic jams

💡 Hot Tip: 📸 No photography, but memories are guaranteed. Dress traditionally, show up early!

- **Sree Muthappan Temple— "Fish, Toddy, and Faith"**

LORD MUTHAPPAN

📍 Parassinikadavu, Kannur, Kerala

🐾 Muthappan—a folk blend of Shiva and Vishnu

🔥 Why It's Cool:

🐟 The only temple where dogs are sacred, fish and toddy are offerings, and Theyyam is part of the daily ritual.

🕉️ Ritual Radar:

🐕 Daily Theyyam performance

🍲 Fish and toddy nivedyam (yes, seriously)

⚡ Power Meter: 9.7/10—Divine rustic with a rebel streak

💡 Hot Tip: 🍲 Try the temple food—it's unique, flavorful, and deeply symbolic.

- **Tali Mahakshetram— "The Scholar's Temple"**

📍 Kozhikode, Kerala

📘 Shiva with a scholarly twist

🔥 Why It's Cool:

🏛 Linked to ancient education and astronomy; once had a Vedic university inside.

🕉 Ritual Radar:

🔭 Festival linked with star signs

📜 Precise timing and rituals rooted in learning

⚡ Power Meter: 8.5/10—Knowledge power level over 9000

💡 Hot Tip: 🧠 Great spot for spiritually inclined nerds. Come with questions!

- **Mookambika Temple— "Goddess of Wisdom and Wow"**

📍 Kollur, Karnataka (near Kerala border)

🪷 Saraswati-Durga combo as Mookambika

🔥 Why It's Cool:

📚 Especially loved by students—seek her blessings before exams or life decisions.

🕉️ Ritual Radar:

📔 Navaratri and Saraswati Pooja are the main events

🌼 Morning darshan feels like a mental clarity boost

⚡ Power Meter: 9/10—Knowledge + shakti = supercharged focus

💡 Hot Tip: 🖊️ Bring your pens and books for a quick blessing before big milestones.

- **Ettumanoor, Vaikom, and Kaduthuruthy— "The Shiva Triad"**

📍 Kottayam District, Kerala

🔱 Three faces of Shiva energy, each in a unique form

🔥 Why It's Cool:

🌌 Tri-temple circuit is said to balance karma if visited before noon in one day.

🕉️ Ritual Radar:

🛕 Start at Kaduthuruthy, then Vaikom, and end at Ettumanoor

🔥 Murals, giant lamps, and mystic vibes

⚡ Power Meter: 10/10—Combo pack = spiritual upgrade unlocked

💡 Hot Tip:⏱️ Early bird gets the blessing. Plan the route to make it in one spiritual sprint.

- **Triprayar Temple— "The Hero Returns"**

📍 Thrissur District, Kerala

🏹 Rama with a twist (has traits of Vishnu and Shiva)

🔥 Why It's Cool:

🔘 Rama here is worshipped post-Ravana war—intense and serene at once.

🕉️ Ritual Radar:

🛕 Part of Nalambalam Yatra (4 Rama temples in 1 day)

🐉 Major events during Karkidakam

⚡ Power Meter: 8.9/10—Rama with mystery energy

💡 Hot Tip: 📅 Ideal for Karkidaka month visits for a dharma detox.

- **Vadakkunnathan Temple— "Shiva's Classic Edition"**

📍 Thrissur, Kerala

🌀 Shiva as a giant lingam covered in ghee

🔥 Why It's Cool:

🎇 Hosts Thrissur Pooram, Kerala's grandest temple festival. Also has zero aggressive temple politics.

🕉️ Ritual Radar:

🕯️ Ghee abhishekam over centuries (never removed!)

🎉 Thrissur Pooram with fireworks and elephants

⚡ Power Meter: 10/10—Ancient + majestic = high-vibe heritage

💡 Hot Tip: 🎆 If you go once, go during Pooram. It's a festival you feel in your bones.

- **Kodungallur Bhagavathy Temple— "Fierce and Female"**

📍 Thrissur District, Kerala

🩸 Bhadrakali in rage-and-rebirth mode

🔥 Why It's Cool:

🪔 Known for the wild Bharani festival with oracles, blood symbolism, and raw spiritual release.

🕉️ Ritual Radar:

🗡️ Kaavu rituals with swords and trance

🩸 Bharani fest = screams, songs, symbolic chaos

⚡ Power Meter: 10/10—Primal power, not for the faint-hearted

💡 Hot Tip: 🧨 Don't go expecting peace. Go expecting raw, sacred energy.

- **Pambumekkatu Mana— "Home of the Snake Spirits"**

📍 Thrissur District, Kerala

🐍 Serpent deities (Nagas) in tantric tradition

🔥 Why It's Cool:

🌿 Sacred groves, rituals for sarpa dosha (serpent curse), and mystical energy everywhere.

🕉️ Ritual Radar:

🌱 Sarpabali rituals in lush groves

🐍 No idol—just nature and vibration

⚡ Power Meter: 9.8/10—Snake energy + nature = a serious spiritual charge

💡 Hot Tip: 🧬 Go with humility, not curiosity. This place is more ancient science than spectacle.

- **Sucheendram Thanumalayan Temple—Trinity in Stone**

📍 Location: Sucheendram, near Kanyakumari, Tamil Nadu

🐾 Main Deity: Thanumalayan—The powerful fusion of Shiva (Sthanu), Vishnu (Mal), and Brahma (Ayan)—One shrine, three divine vibes

🔥 Why It's Cool:

- Musical pillars 🎵 that actually play notes

- 18-foot-tall Hanuman idol 🐒—one of the tallest in India

🕉️ Ritual Radar:

🔱🪷🐍 Rare combined worship of the Trimurti

👐 Open to all genders, castes, and backgrounds

🕊️ The peaceful coexistence of Shaivite and Vaishnavite customs

⚡ Power Meter: 15/10—Where the Trimurti is worshipped as one

💡 Hot Tip: "Worship here is a shortcut—one darshan, three blessings!"

CHAPTER 9 ³/₄
FIELD GUIDE
COMPENDIUM
FOR THE SPIRITUALLY CURIOUS

Chapter 9 3/4: Field Guide Compendium for the Spiritually Curious

Welcome, seeker. You've wandered through stories, chants, scrolls, sages, and maybe even a few squirrel metaphors. Any book that dares to decode Hinduism needs to peek under the hood of its ancient source code.

But why 9 3/4?

If Chapter 9 was your temple tour, think of Chapter 9 3/4 as the hidden, secret platform to board the spiritual express. Inspired by a certain magical train station, this bonus chapter is a cheat-code compendium — packed with emoji scrolls, one-page wisdom bombs, and quick-reference guides to everything from Vedas to vibes. Because sometimes, the fastest way to dharma is through a side door with a sense of humor.

This section is your personal Room of Requirement. Each entry here is short(er), snappy, Hogwarts-approved, and pop-culture powered.

The Vedas: Hogwarts Scrolls & Dojo Manuals

Think of the Vedas as the universe's starter pack scrolls, dropped from the cloud way before you could say "Hey Siri." There are four of them— each with its own magical (and practical) purpose.

The Vedas

- Rig Veda = Dumbledore's playlist + Shifu's mantra board. Packed with hymns and chants — basically ancient Spotify, but with spiritual bass drops.
- Sama Veda = Auto-tuned rituals. Like Hogwarts' chorus club mixed with meditative trance music. Vibe check: strong.
- Yajur Veda = Rituals 101. Step-by-step instructions for sacred ceremonies—kind of like IKEA meets ninja scrolls. No allen keys, just fire altars.
- Atharva Veda = Bikini Bottom survival guide. Home remedies, anti-curse tips, and mantras for dodging shady vibes. Plankton energy, not welcome.

Written in Sanskrit, powered by sound, and coded for conscious living, the Vedas aren't about blind obedience—they are about inner alignment. No commandments. No chosen ones. Just you, the cosmos, and a divine cheat code that helps you live like a wizard, fight like a monk, and vibe like SpongeBob post-karate class.

Vedas Field Guide—Hogwarts x Dojo

Your quick scroll through the four Vedas, powered by emojis, magic, and martial arts wisdom.

Vedas TL; DR

- No commandments. Just cosmic coding
- No gatekeepers. Just inner access
- Read. Chant. Glow up. Repeat

The Upanishads: Inner Magic 101 (No Wand Required)

If the Vedas are like Hogwarts textbooks full of spells and rituals, the Upanishads are what you'd get in Dumbledore's office after hours—when the robes come off and the real wisdom drops.

They are the part where ancient sages stop chanting and start asking,

"Who am I, really?"

"What's the point of all this?"

Think of them as the dojo of inner training — where you don't learn how to fight demons out there, but how to wrestle the ones inside.

Spoiler: most of them look like our own ego.

Instead of potions and rituals, the Upanishads teach you to sit down, shut up (in a good way), and look inward. They whisper:

"Yo, the divinity you are searching for? It is not in the sky. It is you. Always has been."

They are all about Atman = Brahman, a.k.a. your soul is the same Wi-Fi signal as a whole freakin' universe.

No props. No gurus with sparkle filters.

Just breathe, stillness, and a serious spiritual glow-up.

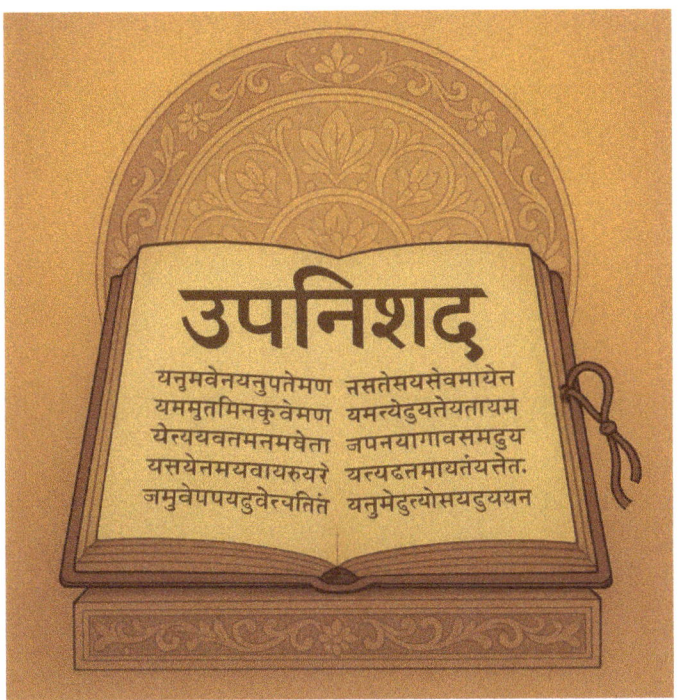

The Upanishad

Upanishad TL; DR

- Drop the noise. Embrace the stillness
- Don't search for magic. *Be• the magic
- The divine isn't out there. It's YOU.

The Gita: Hogwarts x Dojo on the Battlefield of Life

Imagine this: You are Arjuna, a warrior with major impostor syndrome. You are standing in the middle of a massive battlefield (a.k.a. think chaotic life), and suddenly you freeze. Total existential crisis.

Your wand is shaking. Your sword is slipping.

You don't want to fight.

You want to disappear into a blanket burrito.

Enter Krishna — your magical life coach, sensei, and part-time cosmic Uber driver.

He doesn't hand you tissues.

He drops some of the most legendary wisdom in all of history.

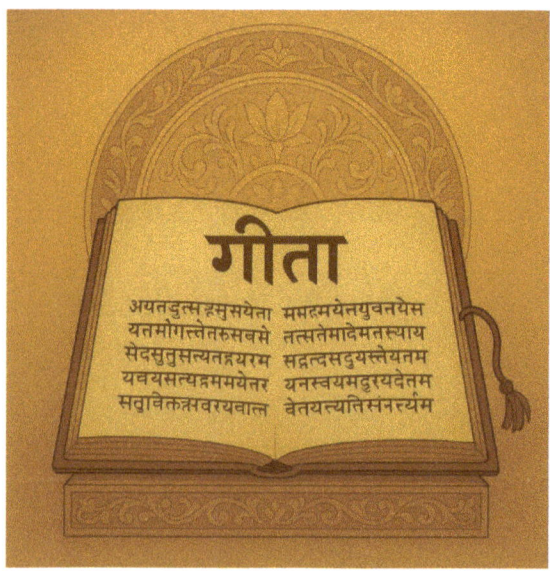

The Gita

Here's the Gita Breakdown

"Do your dharma, Harry."

(Just like Harry had to face Voldemort, we have got a duty—whether it is our job, our truth, or our calling. No ghosting it because it is hard.)

Krishna says, "Act. Don't flinch."

"Don't chase the scoreboard."

(Martial arts 101: You train for the form, not the trophy.)

"Do the action, detach from the results."

You can't control the outcome — only your effort.

"You are not your body, your grades, or your wand skills."

You are Atman — your unshakable, indestructible true self.

Your soul is eternal.

"Multiple paths, one goal."

Whether you are a Bhakti yoga devotee (Hufflepuff energy),

Karma yogi (Gryffindor grind),

or Jnana nerd (Ravenclaw vibes)—

all lead to the same truth: the divine is within.

"Meditate like a ninja, fight like a Jedi."

The Gita isn't about escaping life.

It is about being in the arena, swords drawn, heart calm.

Think Yoda meets Bruce Lee, with a sprinkle of Dumbledore.

Gita TL; DR (Totally Legit Dharma Recap):

- Do what is right—even if it is hard.
- Let go of control.
- Your soul = invincible.
- Pick your spiritual path.
- Inner stillness = ultimate flex.

The Ramayana: When Mr. Nice Guy Goes Full Warrior Monk Mode

Picture this: You are Prince Ram — total Gryffindor vibes — kind, principled, can fight like a Dragon Warrior but chooses peace unless pushed. Then life hits you like a rogue Bludger.

Your dad makes a wild promise (thanks to a stepmom with Umbridge-level energy), and you get exiled for 14 years. You don't throw a fit. You pack your things, bow to duty, and leave behind the throne like a straight-up monk on a side quest.

In the forest, it is not all chill meditation and squirrel befriending. You are out here dealing with shape-shifting demons, forest rogues, and major Death Eater drama. Then bam—your wife, Sita, gets kidnapped by a villain with the brains to fill 10 heads (basically the Voldemort of Lanka, but more strategic and way more dramatic). Time to channel your inner Bruce Lee–meets–Dumbledore.

Enter your ride-or-die: Hanuman — a devoted, tribal warrior willing to cross mountains and oceans for his nice-guy friend and idol. Forget sidekick—this dude is the embodiment of loyalty, with mad parkour and power boost unlocked.

The King and His Loyal Soldier

Whoa, whoa, whoa—pause the playlist and drop the banana chips!

I know what you are thinking:

"Umm… where's Hanuman's tail?!"

Trust me, I didn't Photoshop it out because he failed the jungle dress code. This is still our OG mountain-lifting, Lanka-jumping, full-swag Hanuman — just in a form that might blow your young brain like Thor's hammer at Comic-Con.

Imagine if Kung Fu Panda trained under Yoda, had Hulk's strength, SpongeBob's loyalty, and Harry Potter's sense of destiny — That is Hanuman, tail or no tail.

📍 Don't worry — I have got your confusion bookmarked. There's a legit, deep, "mind = blown" reason for this. Stay tuned. The "tail tale" is coming. (Chapter 13A)

Anyway, together, the two pull off an epic rescue mission that makes the Battle of Hogwarts look like a pillow fight.

You'd think the story ends there — happily ever after, right? Nope.

Even after all that, Ram is judged for one decision—asking Sita to prove her purity, just to silence kingdom gossip.

That move? Controversial.

It broke hearts, sparked debates, and still fuels comment-section wars to this day.

Ram, the OG nice guy, carried the weight of public perception vs. personal truth — like a true tragic hero.

Ramayana TL; DR:

A noble prince gets exiled, slays demons, rescues his queen, and upholds dharma like a spiritual ninja — but still gets side-eyed by society for doing what he thought was right.

He's not perfect. He's human.

And that's what makes the Ramayana hit hard:

It's about staying true to your values 🧭 even when life goes full telenovela.

Moral Takeaway:

- Uphold values, even when it hurts
- Not every hero gets applause
- Dharma is messy—but worth it

The Mahabharata — Family Drama, Battle Trauma, and K-Drama Karma

(Now streaming in your mind's eye—rated PG for Pandava-Grit)

Welcome to the Mahabharata, a.k.a. the ancient Indian epic where everyone's related, no one's chill, and dharma is more confusing than your Hogwarts House quiz results.

☕ So here is the tea:

Two royal cousin gangs:

- The Pandavas = Team Righteous Bros
- The Kauravas = Team Too Many Siblings 🧍🧍🧍🧍🧍...

Fighting over Hastinapura—basically the Iron Throne, but with more elephants and fewer dragons.

Cue 18 days of magical weapons, plot twists, and ghost dads. Yep.

Meet the Main Cast:

- Yudhishthira—The Eldest Pandava, with a virtue so strong that he probably says "please" to mosquitoes before swatting
- Bhima—The muscle. Think Hulk + food blogger
- Arjuna—Bow master with emotional energy. Needs constant pep talks from divinity
- Nakula and Sahadeva—Twins. Pretty. Horse whisperers + quiet geniuses.
- Krishna — Not technically in the fight but totally running the show. Wise, sassy, casually God. Drops the original TED Talk (a.k.a. the Bhagavad Gita) mid-battle while Arjuna has a panic attack. Iconic.

MAHABHARATA

The Mahabharata

What Went Down?

The Pandavas lose everything in a cursed game of dice because, apparently, never trust your shady uncle's dice.

- Exiled
- Return
- Ask nicely for five villages
- Kauravas: "lol no"

Boom: Kurukshetra War begins

Think: Battle of the Department of Mysteries + Endgame + SpongeBob's "Karate Island"

Plot Highlights:

- Arjuna freezes. Krishna drops truth bombs. Arjuna goes full Avatar State
- Bhishma (grand-uncle, 1000% done with everyone) naps on a bed of arrows until the vibes improve
- Draupadi — Wife of all five Pandavas (polyandry and polyepic). Survives humiliation, vows revenge, and draws most satisfaction from the annihilation of the Kauravas
- Karna—Chariot-driving, tragic hero energy. Loyal to the wrong squad but rides with dignity. RIP
  • Duryodhana—Rich kid rage villain. Gets mace-smashed by Bhima after Krishna cheats just a little

The Lesson?

- Karma = ruthless
- Dharma = hard
- Life = gray zone

Even victory feels like defeat when your whole family is gone

Arjuna cries. Yudhishthira almost rage-quits kingship. Krishna gives side-eyes.

🎬 Final Scene:

Years later, the Pandavas walk to heaven.

One by one, they drop like a reality show elimination round

Only Yudhishthira makes it — because ethics never dies

Mahabharata TL; DR:

- Ancient India's Infinity War + Shakespeare + Kung Fu Panda
- Plot armor is fake. Dharma is real.
- Revenge is... complicated.
- Krishna wins Best Supporting God

Moral of the Story?

Even if life feels like a rigged dice game, play with honor, channel your inner Pandava, and always keep Krishna on speed dial.

A Note on Chanting:

Why Chanting Isn't Just You Mumbling Like a Wizard with a Cold

Chanting mantras isn't just making your room echo like Hogwarts during finals.

It is like casting a real-life spell but instead of turning frogs into teacups, you are syncing your body, breath, and brain into beast mode.

Sound = Energy, the original influencer.

The universe literally began with Om — the cosmic "Alohomora" that unlocked existence itself.

That one syllable still ripples through everything — like a sacred Wi-Fi signal connecting you to the divine mainframe.

Mantras are like dojo drills for our nervous system.

When chanted with the right tone and placement (uchcharana sthalashuddhi, for the Sanskrit nerds), they massage our cells, clear mental fog, and reboot chakra OS.

It's the vocal version of Tai Chi, but for your brainwaves.

And when you do this in a temple (basically an energy hotspot) or the Room of Requirement for your soul, it's like putting your phone on a 200% fast charge.

The space amplifies your vibe. You vibrate higher. You glow.

But here's the catch:

- Don't go into full SpongeBob autopilot.
- If you are chanting like a zombie Krabby Patty flipper, it is just noise.
- Do it with intent.
- Feel the vibration.
- Be the wand, not just the wand-waver.

🕉 Mantra TL; DR

- Sound heals.
- Chant clearly.
- Do it with intention.

And please—don't chant like you are sleepwalking in Squidward's apron.

Interlude 2: Temple Tantrums, Tiled Roofs, and Angry Gods

Picture this: I am part of a family temple Trust (capital T, and definitely not always capital trust). Once upon a time, this was a peaceful little shrine built with love and devotion by my legendary Valliamma. Fast forward a few decades, and like any good soap opera, things got hijacked. A group of well-meaning (ish) folks turned it into their own personal stage with themselves as the Management Committee™.

Cut to 40 years later: surprise plot twist! The Trust has finally dusted itself off and found new life, thanks to a few brave warriors who decided enough was enough and brought the temple back to its roots — literally. Now, our "tharavadu" (family) gets to relive the golden days of summer holidays filled with traditions, temple visits, and gossip that tastes better than the prasadam.

But wait — it is never that simple.

Turns out, Ayyappan might be unhappy with his current seating arrangement. There was a full-on spiritual debate over whether he needs a new location, a higher chair, a better view, or a stylish, eco-tiled roof. Also, the main deity, the Goddess, appears to be having an identity crisis—Bhuvaneshwari, according to some, Bhadrakali, according to a few others. Regardless, she has been serving some serious grump energy. Milk has been going bad daily, food is mysteriously spoiling, and someone is clearly playing divine dodgeball with what feels like cosmic banana peels. We have ruled out carelessness because, as you know, that is no longer considered a human trait. And then if this wasn't serious enough, someone decided to look up Vastu-shastra—and BOOM, it all became crystal clear! Ayyappan wanted to move into the Naga corner, the Nagas had put in a request for a transfer to the Rakshas' compound and the poor old Rakshas? Well, we are yet to solve that part.

Oh, and here comes the scandal of the decade: the main priest is not a Brahmin. Gasp. How dare someone from outside the VIP spiritual club lead Vedic rituals—even if he is educated, well-trained, and a graduate of "We Are Rituals" University, with honors in "Mantras and Practical Spirituality".

What is really going on here isn't just divine interior decorating or caste-coded controversies — it is a slow-burning drama that plays out in many temples and family trusts — emotions clashing with logic, tradition wrestling with change, and egos standing taller than temple gopurams.

As for me? I will let this celestial tug-of-war play out until I summon the Thor in me and step in with my Mjölnir. For now, I am just waving my "Team Sanity" flag, cheering on the practical, the logical, and the middle path. It is not easy, but hey, it keeps the spirit alive without setting off theological landmines.

And just for the record—my book was already in the works before this divine drama began. So no, this is not an exposé. It's just… awkward timing. Or divine comedy. You decide.

Section 4:

🔬 Myth-Taken Identities and Ritual Routines

Chapter 10. Welcome to the Templeverse: No Capes, Just Kasavu

Do you ever feel like temple rituals are right out of some ancient Hogwarts curriculum?

Or like Doctor Strange opened a cosmic portal and out popped lamps, coconuts, and barefoot uncles humming Vedic lo-fi?

Welcome to Kerala's spiritual multiverse where everyday customs are low-key sacred scrolls and high-key ancient hacks.

Here, every pooja is a power-up, each lamp is a vibe check, and walking barefoot is both a flex of humility and a bonus acupressure.

From smashing your ego with a coconut (mic drop, but spiritual) to pulling all-nighters for Shiva like it's a cosmic sleepover, you are about to see just how lit (literally) and legit our rituals really are.

And the best part?

No magic wand required. Just a little faith, a lot of lamps, and maybe some prasadam.

🪔 Deeparadhana: When Lamps Do the Talking

You are at a temple. It is serene... and suddenly — bam!

The priest appears with a glowing lamp, swirling it before the deity like a divine light show.

Deeparadhana = fire + faith.

It is the original spiritual spotlight — done not just for vibes, but to invoke presence, energy, and devotion.

In Kerala, it is a full-on visual symphony. The vilakkumadam (lamp platform) glows like mood lighting from a Vedic music video. The act of swirling the lamp? That is aarti — a ritual choreography of light, intention, and surrender.

Next time you see it? Don't just record it for your Insta story. Absorb it. Feel it. Let the light in.

🛈 Vazhipadu: Your Spiritual To-Do List

Vazhipadu is like your devotional Amazon cart — a wish-list of rituals and offerings that gets forwarded to the divine inbox.

Vedi Vazhipadu — The Firecracker Flex (Special mention)

You haven't really been to Sabarimala if your ears didn't get blessed (or mildly assaulted) by the thunderclap of Vedi Vazhipadu. It is the original explosive devotion package: a firecracker ritual where you choose between Cheriya Vedi (small boom) or Valiya Vedi (Avengers-level detonation).

Devotees offer these in meaningful numbers — like one for each family member, or sacred MVPs like 11, 21, 101, or the GOAT: 108. (Because nothing says "divine math" like explosions + numerology.)

And the real star? The loudspeaker announcer (Sabarimala's very own hype man). All day long, he'd boom out firecracker forecasts like:

"36 Valiya Vedi!"

Cue every kid's adrenaline spike. My brothers and I would freeze mid-aravana like Harry spotting a Patronus, eyes wide, waiting for the sky to roar.

It wasn't just noise. It was a ritual. A countdown. A spiritual mic drop that echoed through the hills and your bones.

You offer coconuts, ghee lamps, explosives, Palpayasam, or go full send with Udayasthamana Pooja. You queue, submit your printed slip, and the priest beams your spiritual signal into the cosmos.

But here's the kicker: this isn't bribery, it is barter with the cosmos. You give energy, intent, effort and hope the universe blesses you back. No cashback guarantee, but sometimes... prasadam hits just right.

Maha Shivaratri: The All-Night Inner Reset

It is midnight. You are still awake not because Netflix said, "Are you still watching?" but because the stars are aligned for your spine to become a cosmic antenna.

Myth says Shiva drank poison to save the world. Yogis say this night has a natural upward energy flow.

But wait ⚠️ lying flat during this cosmic alignment might trigger spiritual static: restlessness, low energy, even headaches. Solution? Sit up, light a lamp, and meditate.

You are not just avoiding weird dreams—you are syncing with the universe's firmware update.

🥥 Coconut Smashing: Sacred Power Move

You walk into a temple. You grab a coconut. You slam it down as if you are challenging your GPA to a duel. But plot twist: it is not rage. It is a ritual.

🥥 Coco-note: As a kid, every time I managed to break a coconut (especially when my younger brothers couldn't), I'd proudly and secretly flex and admire my scrawny arms, imagining my biceps to have grown — proof that I was clearly the family's newly anointed muscle god. This went on until my younger brothers grew stronger and showed me that coconut+momentum+granite+gravity ≠ mad muscles.

The shell? Your ego. The inside? Your soul, finally free.

Smashing it = saying "Dear Universe, crack this ego and keep the prasadam." It is a symbolic surrender with snack value.

Some folks go full Hulk—smashing 12 in a row.

It's like CTRL + ALT + DHARMA for the soul — resetting your attitude in one loud, satisfying crunch.

⚖️ Thulabharam: The Divine Weigh-In (Now Featuring Bananas)

Step up to a temple weighing scale as if you're entering the IPL of devotion.

One side: You. Other side: Bananas, sugar, or gold — whatever you promised when you desperately prayed for exam marks, visa approvals, or fewer arguments with your parents.

Balance the scale = full symbolic surrender. Bonus? All that good stuff goes to charity.

And yes, this is the only weigh-in where going heavier might mean you are holier. Devotion > Dumbbells.

Vagacharthu: The OG Divine Mood Diffuser

Smell that sharp, herbal note in the temple? That is Vagacharthu — sacred swag made of vacha root, tied to deities and doors like a spiritual air freshener.

In ancient Kerala, it doubled as a bug repellent, vibe cleanser, and cognitive booster.

Think of it as temple-grade essential oil armor. You are not just smelling devotion — you are inhaling generations of Ayurvedic wisdom. It is Ayurveda meets Febreze — with bonus mosquito block.

Bonus: It is sometimes used for kids with attention issues. Holy focus diffuser, anyone?

🌙 Ekadashi: The Spiritual Detox Day You Didn't Know You Needed

Forget crash diets and "celery juice for the soul" trends—Ekadashi is the OG mind-body-spirit reset button.

Happening twice a month (on the 11th day of each lunar fortnight), Ekadashi is that sacred moment when the universe sends you a cosmic memo:

"Hey, maybe don't eat like it is Onam today."

Why? Because according to yogis and grandmas alike, your body's digestive fire slows down, your mind gets clearer, and the energy around you goes full Zen mode. It is prime time for prayer, meditation, and self-check-ins.

So, what do you do?

- Skip rice (legend says grains absorb extra cosmic energies a.k.a. carbs—and not in a good way)
- Eat lightly or fast completely
- Binge mantras, not Netflix
- Avoid unnecessary drama, scrolling, or shade

Some say that the essence of life, the divine Vishnu, "sleeps lightly" on

Ekadashi—so the vibes are extra peaceful if you tune in.

And no, it is not about starving. It is about clearing space—in your gut, in your thoughts, and in your karma cloud.

So, the next time someone says:

"Fasting is hard." Just smile and say, "so is carrying emotional baggage and spiritual lag. I'm good, thanks."

🐍 Pulluvan Paattu: When Worship Gets a Bit... Hiss-terical

Imagine EDM for serpents. That's Pulluvan Paattu—performed with hypnotic instruments like the pulluva veena and clay pot drums in honor of snake gods.

In Kerala, serpent groves (Sarpa Kavu) aren't scary—they're sacred. And these haunting folk tunes are like nature's Spotify playlist for protection, fertility, and harmony.

It is part ritual, part trance, and totally otherworldly. Just don't expect lyrics you can hum in the shower. It is snake-charming music that hisses blessings at you.

🔥 Chuttu Vilakku: When the Divine Shows Up, You Light It Up

During temple festivals, Kerala's energy bills experience a significant drop because customs like Chuttu Vilakku are an all-lamp-everything extravaganza with no electricity needed.

Ghee lamps encircle the sanctum like cosmic fairy lights, each one lit with devotion, intention, and a touch of spiritual bling.

Each flame = a prayer. Each row = collective glow. Step into that light tunnel and boom—you've entered Devotee Mode: Activated.

🌅 Udayasthamana Pooja: The Ultimate All-Day VIP Pass for the Gods

What is more special than a brunch? An all-day divine spa day

Udayasthamana Pooja = worship from sunrise to sunset. Priests, cooks, and musicians all team up to pamper your chosen deity with baths, songs, feasts, and rituals on loop.

It is devotion dialed up to 100 — and blessings often follow.

You are not just praying. You are curating a full 12-hour vibe for God. Talk about spiritual event planning.

📘 Field Guide to Kerala Temple Rituals – Updated

Ritual	What It Means
🪔 Deeparadhana	Lighting lamps = lighting up your inner wisdom. Spiritual spotlight moment.
🌿 Vazhipadu	Personal prayer package: coconuts, lamps, flowers → blessings & prasadam.
🌙 Shivaratri	One all-nighter worth pulling. Energy alignment + inner clarity.
🥥 Coconut Smashing	Break ego, not fruit. Pride out, surrender in.
⚖ Thulabharam	Get weighed in bananas to show thanks. Drama meets devotion.
🌿 Vagacharthu	Sacred herbal garland = ancient temple diffuser. Clears bad vibes, boosts focus, smells like devotion.
🌙 Ekadashi	The spiritual detox day. Fast, reflect, declutter your karma cloud. Grain-free = mind-free. Vishnu-approved reset ritual.
🐍 Pulluvan Paattu	Snake-worship songs that slither into your soul. Divine hiss vibes.
🔥 Chuttu Vilakku	Surround the temple with lamps. Light up the dark—literally and spiritually.
🍶 Udayasthamana Pooja	All-day temple pampering. You host, god chills, blessings pour.

✏ Bonus: Miracles, Misunderstood: When the Divine Goes Lowkey

One Last Thing Before You Go: Worship a Pipe

Because while we are talking temple vibes, let us also talk about what doesn't qualify as a divine download.

We live in times where people are desperate for a sign from the divine—any sign. A blinking streetlight? Definitely Shiva. A particularly symmetrical potato? Must be Vishnu trying to contact you through carbs.

The problem? We have rebranded "miracle" to mean "spectacle."

Unless there is an ocean parting, a voice thundering from the clouds, or a deity showing up with GPS coordinates, we scroll on and say, "Meh. Not divine enough."

Back in the day, gods were apparently running a full-blown celestial VFX studio—burning bushes, floating chariots, multiplying food like mythological MasterChefs. But ever since science and technology started creeping into human lives? Crickets.

People claim it has been a miracle-dry season for the past 500 years across all religions — drier than a WhatsApp family group without drama.

So, what do humans do?

We start stretching our imagination so far, even Bollywood's like: "Bro ... tone it down."

Take this:

- A broken underground pipe causes water to gush out of a tree in Pune and instantly — BOOM — temple. Worship begins. TikTok videos follow. Probably a local WhatsApp prophecy too.
- Remember the Milk Miracle? Someone strategically placed a bowl under a Ganesh idol, and suddenly it's like, "OMG, he's sipping milk through his trunk!" (Plot twist: capillary action. Science called. It wants its dignity back.)
- And the classic — vibhuti (ash) randomly materializing from a deity's photo in your mom's pooja room. That picture's been there since 1987. Nobody touched it except the dust.

The real miracles?

It's that we have stopped noticing the small ones — the quiet everyday wins that don't trend but totally deserve to:

- Waking up without back pain (shout-out to the mattress gods)
- Still feeling the glow from a basic yoga routine — even post spinal surgery! a.k.a. walking pain-free with balance!
- That one cup of filter coffee that hits harder than therapy
- A loved one's medical results coming back clear (cue happy tears)
- And just... five whole uninterrupted minutes of actual peace before the next ping ruins it

Miracles don't always scream. Sometimes, they whisper in a language we forgot how to hear.

Chapter 11:
Beyond Fairy Tales

What If Myths Were Metaphors?

Chapter 11: Beyond Fairy Tales —What If the Myths Were Metaphors?

A young Hindu's guide to decoding Gods, temple rituals, mythic metaphors, and energy hacks

"Bro, Why Do You Have So Many Gods?" — A Totally Chill Explainer

(Yeah, I touched on this in the Primer. But let's break it down like it is a boss battle.)

So, you are scrolling through your feed, and bam—another meme about Hinduism.

Then someone hits you with:

"Dude, why do you have, like, a thousand gods and goddesses?"

First off: We don't.

Actual answer?

We have got zero gods in the way most people think.

Let me explain—with cartoons, kung fu, and cosmic metaphors, obviously.

It is Not People. It is Power.

In Hinduism, we don't worship people. We worship ideals—personified to make them relatable.

Think: Avengers.

You are not obsessing over Iron Man's suit—you are vibing with his courage, genius, and sacrifice.

Each "god" is like a cosmic profile picture for a quality we want to level up into:

Lakshmi = CEO of abundance and ethical hustle

Shiva = Chill king of focus, transformation, and "let it go" energy

Saraswati = Nerd queen of knowledge, music, and inspired thinking

These aren't sky people on cloud-Wifi. They are vibes with divine swag.

What Makes Someone "Godly"?

Glad you asked, young Padawan.

When someone masters these ideals so deeply — think Kung Fu Panda reaching Dragon Warrior status — we say, "That's divine behavior right there."

Po started off tripping over himself and eating noodles. But once he tapped into his truth (and dumpling-fueled chi), he became who the "Valley of Peace" needed.

Same deal.

Be so wise, fearless, or kind that people say, "You're basically on god mode."

Worship? Nah. It's About the Upgrade.

SpongeBob doesn't meditate under a Bodhi tree, but he does stay joyful, honest, and totally unbothered by Squidward's energy.

Krishna? Teaches us to slay doubts, not cousins.

(Yeah, complex. Covered in Chapter 9 3/4 under Gita and Mahabharata.)

Rama? Walked away from a kingdom because dharma > drama.

We don't have commandments. We have got cheat codes.

Not "believe or else," but "live it, feel it, evolve with it."

The Real Glow-Up

It is not about collecting temple stamps or racking up divine loyalty points.

It is about being a decent human who treats others with respect.

Golden Rule + Inner Kung Fu + Spiritual Wi-Fi = Sanatana Dharma

So next time someone asks, "Why so many gods?"

Just say:

"It is not about how many gods we have. It is about how many versions of our best self we are aiming for."

Mic drop. Namaste. Pass the prasad.

Why Does Your God Have So Many Arms and Heads?

Multitasking at a divine scale needs multi-limbs and parallel processing

In Hinduism, gods and goddesses aren't limited by human bodies. Extra arms? Symbolic. Extra heads? Purposeful.

Think superhero gear, not mythic mutation.

Why All the Extra Limbs?

In our world, multitasking = chips + texting + Kung Fu Panda.

In divine terms? It is protecting, blessing, creating, destroying, guiding, dancing—simultaneously.

- Each arm = one divine action.
- Multiple limbs = multiple apps running on infinite RAM.
- Hindu gods are the original multitools.

And What's with the Extra Heads?

Each head = a unique mode of awareness:

- Wisdom
- Hyper-awareness
- Ego destruction
- Cosmic communication

It is like Google Chrome with 108 tabs open — but no lag.

Shiva's five heads? He's tracking:

- Past
- Present
- Future
- Inner truth
- … and probably your soul's TikTok trends

Hermione needed a Time-Turner to attend two classes.

Brahma said, "Four heads, no Time-Turner needed."

"Time? Space? I invented those."

Doctor Strange opens 14 portals with two hands. Durga fights 10 demons with 10 hands while riding a lion. In full glam.

Now that's a real Endgame.

TL; DR:

Not weird. Just wired for infinity.

Cosmic Multitasking: Activated (Because "doing it all" isn't just a mom superpower — it is divine protocol)

🔶 Status: Multitask unlocked. Mind blown. Blessings incoming x10.

Why Are Your Gods Blue?

Cosmic Cool or Avatar Mode Activated?

Let's face it: Hindu gods are straight-up icons. But there is one question that even your textbook avoids like it is an awkward aunt at a wedding:

"Why are they all… blue?"

Nope. It is much, much cooler than that. Enter the Divine Hex Code: #SpiritualBlue

- Blue isn't just a color — it is a vibe. A cosmic flex. A spiritual power filter.
- In Hinduism, blue = infinity. The sky is blue. The ocean is blue. You know what else is blue? Calm. Depth. Limitless energy.

So, when Vishnu, Krishna, or Shiva shows up looking like they just walked off a moonlit runway — it is not skin tone. It is soul tone.

💡 The Real Takeaway

Blue in Hindu iconography =

- Calm in the chaos
- Depth in action
- Infinite but approachable
- Powerful yet fluid

TL; DR: Divine = avatar blue. Not a filter, but a frequency.

Why the bling at the temple? (Hint: It's not for the selfies)

💎 Bling It On: Why We Wear Jewelry to Temples

(Because sometimes, the sparkle is spiritual)

So, you are stepping into a temple, and suddenly it is less about the dress code and more about divine fashion week. Gold chains, nose rings, anklets, bangles, earrings... Is this a place of worship or a celestial runway?

Short answer: Yes. It is both. Precious metals absorb energy.

Wearing jewelry to temples isn't just about flexing grandma's heirlooms. It is a deep, old-school way of saying:

"I'm dressing up for the divine. I respect this energy. And yes, I sparkle with purpose."

Long Answer: Temples are cosmic charging stations, not fashion runways. Jewelry —especially gold and silver— acts like energetic conduits. Worn on pulse points, they sync your body with temple vibrations. Mantras activate the space, and your bangles tune you in.

MYTH

WHY WEAR JEWELRY TO TEMPLES?

SCIENCE

TEMPLES ARE ENGINEERED ENERGY CENTERS. SHLOKAS ACTIVATE SUBTLE SOUNDS, AND GOLD & SILVER ABSORB POSITIVE ENERGY

Spiritual Armor, Not Just Accessories

Think of it like this:

- Harry Potter had his lightning scar and Invisibility Cloak.
- Tony Stark had his Arc Reactor glowing through his chest.
- Po wore the Dragon Scroll in his soul,

but we mere mortals? We channel power through anklets and earrings.

The Meaning Behind the Sparkle

- Earrings—Not just pretty: they touch acupressure points linked to wisdom and clarity. Basically, your lobes are little GPS satellites for focus.
- Finger rings—Channel energy through nerve endings. (Also great for subtle flexes during namaste.)
- Anklets—Every step you take becomes a musical offering. Jingle = devotional playlist.
- Head ornaments—Focus energy on the ajna chakra (third eye). Because even your thoughts want to look good in front of the deity.

Bonus: Gold is considered pure, silver is cooling, and both are fabulous at any angle.

TL; DR: Jewelry = spiritual antenna. Not style, but signal.

Why ring the bell before entering?

🔔 Ring It Like You Mean It: The Real Reason We Hit That Temple Bell

(Spoiler: It is not to wake up the gods—it is to wake you up)

So, you are entering a temple. You walk in quietly, peacefully... and suddenly someone near the door goes full Thor on a brass bell.

CLAAAAANGGGG!

Your soul jumps, your spine straightens, and your monkey brain goes,

"Whoa. What dimension did I just enter?"

Exactly. Welcome to the sound check of the sacred.

WHY RING YOU UP BEFORE ENTERING A TEMPLE?

- **It's to wake you up**
  Activates your brain's alpha state – focused and calm

  Drowns out mental noise and distractions

Resonates throughout the temple
Prepares body and mind to align with the temple's vibration

Why the Bell, Though?

It is not for acoustics. It is a ritual sonic boom with serious spiritual swag. It is to reboot your brain — not to wake the deity. Temple bells emit healing frequencies (around 528 Hz, also called the 'love frequency') that calm your mind, cleanse your energy, and prep you spiritually.

The bell is your portal pass. When you ring it:

- You shift from outside noise to inner silence
- You say, "Hey mind, stop scrolling"
- You sync up with the frequency of the divine

Basically, it is Airplane Mode for your thoughts. Avengers-Style

Ancient texts say the echo should last long enough to calm your thoughts. Science says the frequencies can actually affect your brainwaves. Elders typically say, "Just ring it and stop asking questions."

In Kerala, they used to tell us that only Brahmins can ring the bell! (and if someone dares to, give that bell the loudest "clang" ever)

So Next Time...

Don't just tap the bell as if you are afraid to disturb someone. Ring it like Po found his inner peace, like Thor just landed, or like Hermione finally got into the Restricted Section.

It is not noise. It is the password to presence.

🔟 Status: Mind awakened. Thoughts silenced. Entry granted.

TL; DR: Bell = Awaken the soul.

Why walk barefoot in temples?

👣 The Sacred Sole Story

You take off your shoes. You enter the temple. Your feet hit the cool stone floor, and you

"Am I underdressed... or is this an ancient Wi-Fi connection for my soul?"

Plot twist: It's the second one.

The Temple Floor = Nature's Charging Pad

Think of temple floors as ancient Earth-powered chargers. Those stone slabs? They are not just decorative—they are direct spiritual USB ports connected to the cosmic motherboard.

There's Science Too!

- Grounding/Earthing: Science says walking barefoot balances your body's electrons and reduces inflammation. So basically, barefoot = superhero recovery protocol.
- Sensory Awareness: When your soles touch sacred ground, your soul also pays attention. You move slower, more mindful — like Doctor Strange in slow-motion time-loop mode.

- Cleanliness + Humility: You leave ego, dirt, and rubber soles at the gate. That's spiritual protocol 101. Hogwarts probably has a charm for this, but we just use coconut husk doormats.

What's the Real Deal?

Temples are sacred spaces — like natural Wi-Fi zones for the spirit. Shoes block that signal with a layer of ignorance (and mud).

Going barefoot is your way of saying:

"Hey Divine Energy, it's me—raw, respectful, and ready to download blessings."

So Next Time...

...someone asks why you are walking barefoot in a temple, just smile and say:

"Because even the Avengers remove their armor before they meditate."

Or better yet, pull a Po and say, "Inner peace starts at the toes."

Status: Connected. Grounded. Spirit loading... 100%.

Temples are built on geomagnetic hotspots. Stone floors store ritual energy. Barefoot contact = grounding + recharge. Ayurveda calls it marma point activation.

TL; DR: No shoes = cosmic foot spa.

Why offer your hair at temples?

Hair Today, Dharma Forever: Why We Go Bald at Temples

(Or as we call it, the Sacred Buzzcut of Surrender)

So, you walk into a temple, and suddenly, there is someone sitting as if they're in a divine salon—getting their head shaved while chanting prayers and casually manifesting spiritual upgrades. And you think:

"Wait... did this person just trade shampoo for moksha?"

Yes. Yes, they did.

The Dharma of the Barber Blade

Tonsure, or offering your hair to the deity, isn't just about embracing the egghead look. It is about letting go — ego, vanity, that one cowlick you could never tame. Po had to let go of his dumpling obsession to unlock chi.

What's Really Going On?

- Hair = Ego Threads
- The more hair, the more care. But when you let it go? BAM — emotional declutter.

- Sacrifice that matters. We can drop coins in a hundi. Or offer a literal piece of our self. There is something raw, real, and powerful about saying, "Dear deity, here is my head. My doubts. My pride. My dandruff. All yours."
- Equality at Its Finest
- Rich, poor, young, old — everyone looks the same post-tonsure: like a humble devotee with no filter and zero hairstyle drama. That is anti-ego Level 3000.

So Next Time...

...someone asks why folks are going bald at temples, tell them:

"Because it is hard to carry the weight of the universe and a salon blowout."

Or:

"It is not hair loss. It is karmic lightening."

🔋 Status: Ego dropped. Head cooled. Dharma fully uploaded.

Hair = vanity. Tonsuring = surrender. Temples like Tirupati or Palani use it as a ritual of renewal, humility, and vow-keeping.

TL; DR: Buzz cut = ego drop + gratitude flex.

Why do temples face East and have giant gopurams?

Why Temples Face East: Cosmic Feng Shui or Divine GPS?

(Because even the gods like a good sunrise)

You walk into a temple, take your shoes off, and notice something... predictable. The temple's main entrance? Yup—always facing East. Like it is allergic to the west or just really into mornings.

But it is not a design coincidence or Vastu obsession. It is ancient energy engineering, baby.

So... Why East?

Because the East = sunrise = life force energy.

In Hindu dharma, the sun (Surya) is a symbol of divine consciousness, clarity, and the ultimate wake-up call.

Facing East means:

- You literally walk toward the light
- You start your prayers with the universe's daily "Hello, world."
- You get that vitamin D and divine darshan in one go

Why do temples have gopurams and face east?

Gopurams: giant antennas to the universe

Facing east: because temples like sunrise too

Basically, the East-facing temple is nature-approved, sun-synced, and spiritually solar-powered.

Bonus: East Is Symbolic Too!

- East = birth, beginnings, awakening
- Sunrise = new hope, clear mind, fresh dharma downloads
- Facing East in prayer = aligning your inner self with the light

It is not superstition. It is sunlight-level logic. Temples aren't just built—they are calibrated.

So Next Time...

...you wonder why the sanctum doesn't face your house or Instagram reel angle, just remember:

"The gods don't need filters—they have the sun."

Or "When the door faces the dawn, your soul walks into light."

🪔 Status: Spiritual compass locked. Facing light. Inner sunrise loading.

East = sunrise = solar power. Gopurams = divine data towers pulling in cosmic energy.

Architecture wasn't just dramatic—it was aligned with planetary math.

TL; DR: Temples face East to sync you with the sun.

Why can't I touch the deity?

Hands Off, Humans: Why You Can't Touch the Deity

(Because this isn't a selfie booth—it's sacred bandwidth)

So, you walk into a temple, do a full pranam, get hit by that divine glow, and your hand starts twitching like, "Should I... just a little boop on Krishna's toe? A friendly pat on Ganesha's belly?"

STOP. Right. There.

Why No Touchy-Touch?

The deity isn't a statue. It is activated divine energy. Once consecrated, that idol becomes a hotspot of cosmic level shakti. You are not just in front of a sculpture—you are in the presence of an antenna transmitting soul-grade Wi-Fi from the divine source.

So, when they say, "don't touch," what they mean is:

"Please don't poke the universe while it's doing important downloads."

We would not randomly try to high-five Vision's Mind Stone, would we? Or tap Thor's hammer jokingly, with our foot.

Similarly, deities are basically in god mode 24/7. You are welcome to admire, pray, connect — but you don't just walk up and do a finger boop.

Remember when Po tried to snatch the Dragon Scroll before he was ready? It didn't work.

Mastery (and access) takes reverence. Touching the deity without the correct ritual context is like trying to unlock your destiny using a chopstick.

So, What's the Real Deal?

- Boundaries = Respect
- Vibrations Matter
- Access Is Earned

Priests go through purification rituals before performing archana or abhishekam and are trained to interact with these prathishtas (idols) — like engineers handling high voltage. You skipping in post-chai with oily fingers? Not part of the plan. Touching a Pratishtha without ritual purity is like entering a sterile lab wearing beach sandals. Energetically? It's a biohazard.

So Next Time...

...you get the urge to poke Parvati's cheek or fist-bump Hanuman, just remember:

"This isn't Build-a-God Workshop—it is sacred ground."

Or: "Touch with your heart. Not your fingers."

🟧 Status: Divine respect updated. Vibes unbroken. Soul contact = still 100%.

TL; DR: Divine power = hands-off. Watch, don't zap.

Why is the sanctum so dark and cool?

The Dark Room of Dharma: Why Hindu Temples Have Chill Cores

Step into a Hindu temple and you will notice something strange. As you move past the blaring drums, bright lamps, and chatty uncles, you arrive at the garbha griha—the sanctum sanctorum. It is cool. It is dark. It is quiet. Basically, it is the temple's "Do Not Disturb" mode.

But why, you ask? Buckle up, Padawan

The Mood Is Intentional

The garbha griha isn't where you party. It is where you plug in. Think of it as:

- The temple's spiritual battery pack
- The mind palace of the divine
- A sensory detox zone

You leave the chaos at the door and step into the eye of the storm. It is where stillness speaks and the divine doesn't shout— it whispers.

Why the Cool and Dark?

- Darkness = Focus Mode

It is harder to get distracted by your cousin's new outfit or a monkey stealing coconuts when you can't see anything but the deity. It is like the Room of Requirement in Harry Potter, but the only thing you require here is attention.

- Coolness = Calm Vibes Only

Stone walls, minimal ventilation, zero fluorescent lights. This place isn't trying to be an AC room — it just knows how to vibe naturally. Even Iron Man's Arc Reactor would chill out here.

- Inner Peace Zone

What's Really Happening?

You are not just standing in a dark cave. You are stepping into the womb of energy (garbha = womb). The idea is simple—just like life begins in a silent, protected womb, your spiritual transformation begins in this sacred space.

So Next Time...

...you visit a temple and step into the cool, dark heart of it, remember: you are not entering a room. You're entering a dimension. One where you... find yourself

🟥 Status: Sanctuary unlocked. Noise canceled. Soul initiated.

TL; DR: Garbhagriha = Soul's airplane mode.

Why do Pradakshina (walking in circles)?

Why do we walk in slow, meaningful circles around deities like we are trying to confuse a GPS signal? It is called pradakshina, and no — it is not because we forgot where the temple exit is. It is because in Hindu tradition, the divine is the center of your universe, and you revolve around it like the Earth around the sun, or Tony Stark around his Arc Reactor. Think of it as sacred orbiting. Harry Potter would call it a "protective enchantment circle." Master Shifu would say, "Inner peace, one step at a time."

And if you are thinking, "But why always clockwise?"— well, that is the dharma direction. It is like saying, "Hey God, I got your right side because it is auspicious, respectful, and also I don't want to accidentally insult a celestial being with a bad U-turn." So yeah, it is not aimless pacing, it is a spiritual power walk like orbiting the sun. The sanctum is the energetic core, and you revolve to absorb, sync, and humble yourself.

TL; DR: Pradakshina = Boosting Wi-Fi signal by orbiting the deity.

Note: Why don't we go full circle around Shiva?

Okay, but what if the ritual literally breaks the rule? Welcome to Shiva's pradakshina —where *not* completing the circle is the whole point.

Because even the god of transformation comes with a "handle with care" label. Unlike other deities, Shiva's energy isn't just about peace and blessings — it includes the raw power of dissolution, transformation, and moksha (liberation). At the back of his sanctum lies the Guhya Sthana, the secret exit zone for karmic energy and spiritual "deaths." Walking behind Shiva = stepping into that portal zone. Ancient warning system? Maybe. Metaphysical boundary? Definitely. Most devotees stop at 3/4 of the circle and return, symbolizing that some mysteries — like death, liberation, or Shiva's full nature — are not meant to be casually circled.

🌟 BONUS VIBE ALERT: Shiva is also the only deity where *not finishing* a ritual is the ritual.

TL; DR: With Shiva, don't go full circle. Life's biggest truths are meant to be felt, not followed like a map.

Final Thought:

So next time you are in a temple, don't just look around — look through it. Each bell ring, barefoot step, or golden glimmer isn't just for show.

It is a breadcrumb trail left by generations of spiritual hackers who figured out how to vibe with the cosmos.

Hinduism didn't give you commandments. It gave you cheat codes. And guess what? You just unlocked a few.

CHAPTER 12:

From Om to OMG—

Hindu Rites of Passage from Rice Balls to Moksha

CHAPTER 12: FROM OM TO OMG

🥣 Hindu Rites of Passage from Rice Balls to Moksha

*Also known as "Dharma and the Chamber of Samskaras" *

This chapter is your Dharma Diaries — a guide to growing up Hindu without losing your chill.

Imagine if life came with a cosmic GPS. And every time you hit a major milestone — bing! — a spiritual "You Are Here" sign popped up to guide your next move. Like Dumbledore whispering, "Ah, another soul prepares for greatness…"

🍃 That's basically what samskaras are.

In Hinduism, especially in Kerala, samskaras are like the Infinity Stones of life stages—from your first cry to your final bow. They're spiritual save points. You don't just grow up you *level up*.

These rites aren't just about mantras, incense, or aunties with opinions. They are soul-training checkpoints. Dharma tune-ups. Black-belt tests in the art of living with meaning.

So, let's roll out the rice mats, grab our mantra scrolls, and enter the sacred dojo of growing up Hindu.

👶 Namakarana: When the Baby Gets a Name — and Maybe a Destiny Too

"Every hero needs a name."— Kung Fu Panda Scrolls

Let's be honest: babies are born with a lot of mystery. They cry, they sleep, they squirm—but who are they, really?

That is where Namakarana swoops in like Professor McGonagall with a quill and parchment. It is the baby's first official identity spell where your name gets picked not just because it sounds cute, but because it aligns with the stars.

In Kerala, it usually happens on the 11th or 12th day, or on a date approved by the Hogwarts... I mean, astrology council. A priest, elders, and aunties with serious Sorting Hat energy gather around. The father, or sometimes the mother's brother, leans in and whispers the name three times into the baby's right ear.

Cue soft lamps, mantras, and blessings.exe loading...

Namakarana = Passport + First Ninja Belt

Your name becomes your ID tag, your battle cry, and your first pose in the cosmic sparring arena.

⚪ Annaprashana: The Baby's First Official Bite

"With great food comes great responsibility."

If Namakarana is your first "Accio Name!" moment, Annaprashana is "Lumos Taste Buds!"

Usually held around the 6th month, this is when babies are introduced to solid food — often sweet rice like payasam. If you are lucky, it happens at a temple like Guruvayur, where the vibe is full-on Hogwarts + Diwali feast.

Parents, grandparents, and 14 people recording it on smartphones gather around. Whoever gets the honor of feeding the first bite earns +100 karma points.

Beyond the adorableness overload, Annaprashana is like handing Po from Kung Fu Panda his first dumpling: You are not just eating. You are entering sacred culinary combat.

✍️ Vidyarambham: The Day You Start Adulting... with Alphabets

Vidyarambham means the Beginning of Knowledge, a.k.a. your official entry into the League of Learners.

Held on Vijayadashami, this is where your brain gets its first push-up. You write "Om Hari Shree Ganapataye Namah" in raw rice in an "uruli" (a traditional, circular vessel made of bronze), or sometimes directly on the child's tongue with a gold ring.

Think of it as getting your first magic wand, but instead of casting spells, you start spelling. That uncle guiding your hand? Total Mr. Miyagi vibes.

It is your first day at Jedi Academy, Hogwarts, and Avenger boot camp, rolled into one.

🧵 Upanayanam: The Thread That Tied... and Then Excluded

"With great thread comes great... confusion?"

Once upon a time, Upanayanam was the sacred thread ceremony for all students of Vedic wisdom, a black-belt moment in soul training.

But then, like an exclusive superhero club that forgot its origins, it became limited to Brahmins. The poonool turned into a "Members Only" tag instead of a spiritual equalizer.

Let's just say: the ancient rishis probably didn't envision the thread as a barrier spell. They meant it as a signal for higher learning; not a VIP lanyard at a gatekept yagna.

✏️ True Story Time (a.k.a. How I Was Denied)

Here is a twist in this thread business: Some non-Brahmins found an "eye-of-the-needle-sized" loophole in this custom and my grandfather was one of the few to "thread" this needle. Belonging to the Kochi royal family of Thripunithra (a place near Kochi), he wore the sacred thread, just because ...

As a child, I noticed this and, of course, I had to raise this with the elders.

"Can I have one too?" I asked.

I was told I was not qualified to wear one because of my "Nair" status, though the descendant of a Prince. Tsk tsk!! But aren't the Nairs elite? Yes, but not that much... was the answer. Maybe for my 60th birthday, I will get Master Shifu's blessings and sport one... just because...

💍 Marriage: When Two Families (and Their WhatsApp Groups) Become One

"You are now bound by sacred vows… and joint Google calendars."

The Vivaha samskara is when you officially unlock Grihastha Ashrama — the stage of life where you adult hard.

You and your partner become a spiritual tag team — Tony and Pepper, Ron and Hermione, Shiva and Parvati. Your teamwork is tested not just in love but in laundry, leaky roofs, and late-night mantra chants.

Marriage is less about dramatic Bollywood music and more about perfecting your co-op moves in the big Dharma game.

🔮 Astrology, Dosham, and Cosmic Intervals

In Kerala, astrology is like the Daily Prophet meets Fitbit. Your jathakam (horoscope) = cosmic report card.

- Chowa Dosham (Mars): Like Hulk mode — too much fire.
- Drishti (Evil Eye): Like a sneaky Dementor. Zap!
- Eclipses: Cosmic maintenance breaks. No sparring. Just meditate, hydrate, and reset your chi like you're Iron Man upgrading the suit.

In Kerala, astrology isn't just woo-woo wizardry. it is practically a background check for your soul. Parents won't even schedule a haircut without checking planetary moods.

Mars (a.k.a. Chowa Dosham)? That guy throws punches into your love life, your housewarming, or your career goals. Venus in retrograde? Get ready for exes, existential crises, and maybe explosive dosha drama.

And don't even get us started on Drishti (evil eye), that spiritual sneak attack that your grandma claims ruined your exam score, your skin, and your sambhar.

Eclipses? They are not just pretty sky events. They are cosmic "Do Not Disturb" signs. You are supposed to stay indoors, avoid food, and not make any major life moves unless you want Mercury to roast you alive.

✨ Bonus Level: Nakshatras (star constellations) are like your Hogwarts houses.

Are you an Ashwati (fast starter)? A Bharani (emotional tank)? A Pooram (natural performer)? Your nakshatra gives you superpowers and side quests. Just don't use them to win arguments with your siblings.

So yeah — astrology isn't just a vibe. It is a full-on celestial life management app with updates every lunar cycle.

🪶 Death Rituals and Shraddha: Bowing Out Like a Master

In Sanatana Dharma, death isn't the end. It is your final boss-level completion screen. The soul has completed this round of training.

- Antyeshti = final rites.
- Shraddha = remembrance ceremony.

You don't vanish. You phase-shift.

Those who remain carry on the flame, like Harry holding the Resurrection Stone, remembering the ones who guided him.

You bow out not in fear, but in mastery. Like a Jedi. Or a grandmaster turtle.

🧘 Final Word

Live like a seeker, train like a monk, fight like a warrior.

Your rituals aren't just customs; they are ancient moves in the martial art of meaning. You have got more than traditions. You have got a cosmic dojo, a wand of wisdom, and a battle cry made of mantras.

So go forth, channel your inner Avenger, your inner Po, your inner Krishna. Because growing up Hindu? It is not just spiritual.

It's superpowered.

Hindu Rites of Passage — One-Page Field Guide

The Dharma Dojo Checklist

Hindu Samskaras – Training Montage for the Soul

🦋 Ritual	📅 When	🔍 What	🔴 Why
🔔 Namakarana (Naming Ceremony)	11th/12th day or astrologically aligned	Whispering the baby's name in the ear	It's the baby's cosmic login and identity belt
🍚👶 Annaprashana (First Food Ceremony)	6th month (boys), 5th/7th (girls)	First spoon of sweet rice	Training begins with taste—and blessings
✏️📚 Vidyarambham (Start of Learning)	Vijayadashami	Writing in rice or on tongue with gold	The mind's first kata—learning begins
🧵 Upanayanam (Sacred Thread)	Traditionally in youth	Donning the thread for spiritual schooling	Once inclusive; now controversial
❤️💍 Vivaha (Marriage)	Adulthood	Sacred union and adulting level-up	Becoming life-long sparring partners
🔮⚠️ Astrological Conditioning	At birth, during milestones	Jathakam, doshams, and dos & don'ts	Avoiding cosmic curveballs
🕯️🙏 Antyeshti & Shraddha (Final Rites)	End of life & annual observances	Departure rituals and remembrance	A graceful master's exit—until next round

Pro Tip: Every ritual is a checkpoint in your soul's training montage.

INTERLUDE 3: 🪄 TRUE STORY TIME (A.K.A. HOW I BEAT THE STARS)

So, here's a cosmic joke straight from my childhood: our family's go-to astrologer — the one who had divine approval from Amma and grandparents — took one look at my jathakam and declared, "He is going to be a doctor like his father!"

Now, plot twist — I didn't like Biology all that much. Like, full-on Voldemort-level loathing. The only thing worse? Math!!! 😱

Back then, society had only two "acceptable", "successful" male character builds: Medicine or Engineering. If you didn't pick one of these two, you were spiritually downgraded with the curse that no beautiful, educated girl would give you a second look!! Law or Arts apparently meant zero respect and a lifetime of "But, why?"

And being the little rebel Slytherin that I was, I wasn't about to let some zodiac-wielding "panicker" (astrologer) decide my destiny.

So what did I do? I chose Engineering although my love was Arts. Powered through the Maths somehow. Didn't explode a lab (actually, there was one instance when I did, but that was in college and the teacher liked me, so I survived!!). Didn't become that great an engineer, but more importantly, didn't become a doctor either.

Mic drop!! Me 1— Astrologer 0.

Moral? Stars may shine, but you still get to drive the spaceship.

Chapter 13: Sacred Side Streets — Stories, Rituals, and Ridiculously Real Family Drama

Welcome to Chapter 13, or should we say, Chapters 13A and 13B. Yes, I've done the unthinkable. Doubled down on the number everyone else runs from like it's Voldemort's phone number. While the Western world clutches their pearls over 13 — blaming it for everything from Judas' dinner RSVP faux pas to Loki's Valhalla crash-landing (shout out to Marvel for immortalizing that chaos) — we in the East see no such drama.

Hinduism casually slides in a 13th month now and then (Adhik Maas, meaning extra month) like it is no big deal. Bonus month? More time for mantras, dharma points, and cosmic clean-up. Meanwhile, buildings in the West pretend floor 13 doesn't exist, like it is a cursed level in a Harry Potter dungeon or a deleted Avengers timeline.

So yeah, I added two Chapter 13s. Not because I am summoning Deadpool to prank the multiverse or because SpongeBob wore his bad-luck pants again. But because rebellion is sacred, and 13 deserves a comeback tour. We don't flinch at 13—we honor it, we live it, we even chant through it like it is poetic justice—with Sanskrit subtitles and a Chuck Norris-style, roundhouse kick from Po.

Consider this your permission slip to un-cancel the number 13.

Let's roll.

CHAPTER 13 A:
Stories We Grew Up With

-Myths That Live in Our Homes

Chapter 13 A: Stories We Grew Up With — Myths That Live in Our Homes

Every Malayali household has that one person who treats chai time like a Marvel post-credit scene reveal.

You didn't ask for it — but BOOM — suddenly it's "mythology hour."

From Ganesh and his elephant head, to Hanuman's mid-jump bout with the Chayagrahini Rakshasi, and how Yakshis haunted forests and preyed on the "innocent".

> And let us not even start on Kuttichathan, a.k.a. Kerala's very own supernatural prankster who lurks in corners just to make sure you finish your homework *and• drink your milk.

Because let's be honest, only we Malayalis could put the "super" into the "natural" and make the spirit world sound like an extended Avengers universe run by grandmas.

This chapter? We are about to go full Kung Fu Panda meets Kerala folklore — taking ancient legends, giving them a broomstick ride through Hogwarts logic, and wrestling them to tap out with a well-timed cultural kimura.

These iconic tales aren't just cool campfire material. They secretly explain a LOT about our daily customs, rituals, and homegrown superstitions.

⚖️ We are not ranking them. Just decoding them with a pinch of science, a dash of logic, and a whole lot of love for magical realism done Malayali-style.

So, grab your payasam, find a comfy floor mat, and get ready— because these myths didn't just survive... they evolved.

Daruka Vadham: When Kali Went Full Endgame

Okay, so here is my personal favorite with a cup of filter coffee and ready-to-dunk Britannia biscuits.

There once was this villain named Daruka — grade A toxic energy, like if Voldemort, Thanos, and every bad guy from a Kung Fu Panda sequel merged into one. The dude was so evil that the universe basically said, "Nope. Hard stop."

Enter: Goddess Kali, the ultimate boss-level warrior goddess. She rolled in full Fury Mode, ready to delete Daruka from existence. But plot twist! Daruka had a super annoying magical insurance policy:

If even a drop of his blood hit the ground, a thousand Daruka clones would spawn.

(So basically, a demonic version of "Hydra"; cut one head, a thousand grow back. Hail... No thanks.)

Even Kali, with her 18 arms, chakra-charged weapons, and battlefield rage was like: "Yo, this is getting out of hand. Literally."

But here's where she pulls a GOAT move

She extends her tongue like a cosmic magic carpet and slurps up every drop of Daruka's blood before it can hit the Earth. No blood, no clones, no sequel. Boom. Mission Daruka Vadham: Accomplished.

Now, do I think this actually happened? Like, in full CGI slow-motion with a tongue the size of a yoga mat? Of course not.

But metaphorically? Oh yeah.

It is basically Dharma's way of saying:

"If someone causes massive harm, even their influence — every drop of it — needs to be wiped clean from the ecosystem."

Kali wasn't just eliminating the villain, she was canceling his ideology, his fan base, and his toxic ripple effect like she was running divine malware clean-up.

This story? It was a top five banger in Valliamma's mythological mixtape.

And that, my dharma-curious friends, is the vibe of this book:

- Not myth for the sake of fantasy—but stories that serve truth, decoded and reloaded for modern minds.
- No superstition.
- No sci-fi.
- No eyerolls.

Just timeless wisdom, told with a twist.

Busting the Monkey Myth: The Real Hanuman

Hanuman is not just your average mythological monkey swinging around in kids' storybooks. In fact, calling him "just a monkey" is like calling Thor's hammer "just a mallet."

Yes, Hanuman shows up in the Ramayana with flying powers, mountain-lifting strength, and legendary loyalty. He even pops up for a cameo in the Mahabharata like a Marvel end-credits scene. But here's the plot twist—Hanuman is way more Kung Fu Panda than Curious George.

Let's get it straight: The word "Vanara" isn't Sanskrit for "monkey." It actually comes from "Vana" (forest) and "Nara" (man), meaning "forest-dwelling people." Think of them as early indigenous tribes, rockin' wild hair, beastly strength, and animal totems. The poets and

Vedic authors who came later might've gone full Pixar and animalized them for dramatic flair.

So, who really *was* Hanuman?

Cultural Connector: Hanuman represents the ultimate tribal-to-divine upgrade. From jungle strength to cosmic dharma, he's the real bridge-builder between castes, cultures, and inner callings.

Physical Specimen: His speed and agility earned him the nickname "son of the wind god", with yogic mastery and boundless strength. He was like Flash doing Pranayama. Total yogi vibes.

Simian Super Strength: Lifting mountains before it was cool. (Eat your heart out, Hulk.)

Master of Discipline: While Harry Potter was still figuring out Expelliarmus, Hanuman had already mastered Brahmacharya and shapeshifting. Total Gryffindor-Slytherin-Ravenclaw-Hufflepuff combo energy.

> Devotion King: He wasn't just serving Rama—he *embodied•
> Seva (selfless service). Loyalty Level: Avengers Assemble.

So next time someone says, "He's just a monkey," correct them, and drop this truth bomb: That's like saying Iron Man is just a guy in a suit. Or Po is just a fat panda. He was a lot of things combined, but he was definitely NOT a monkey! Behind this hero is a trailblazer. Behind the roar is reason. Hanuman is what happens when raw wildness meets ultimate purpose. Hanuman isn't a cartoon. He's a constellation of strength, spirit, and soul.

Jai Hanuman!

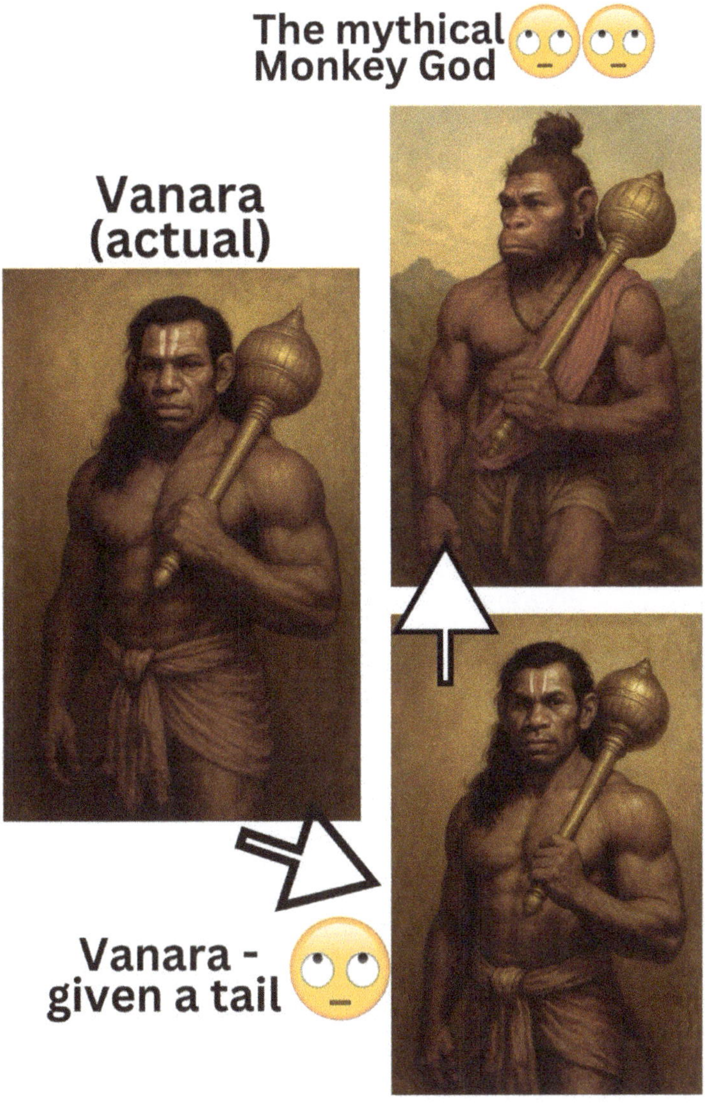

The mythical
Monkey God

Vanara
(actual)

Vanara -
given a tail

The Real Story Behind Ganesha's Elephant Head

Okay, so you have seen Ganesha before — from calendars to the tiny figurine on the dashboard, or in that one temple with really good payasam. He is the one with the round belly, sweet smile, and yep, an Elephant Head.

But why does Ganesha have an Elephant Head? Is it just mythology being extra? Or is there something deeper (and cooler) going on?

Let us rewind to the OG tale—and trust me, it's got EVERYTHING: family drama, mistaken identity, ancient surgery, and a wild twist ending that could rival a Harry Potter plot twist.

Meet the Ganas: Shiva's Squad of Misfits

Before we get to the head swap, you need to meet the Ganas.

You'd expect the mighty Shiva, cosmic destroyer and Nataraja extraordinaire, to roll with gods, sages, and maybe a few Avengers. Nope. His ride-or-die crew? A bunch of misfits. Think: Hogwarts House-elves meets SpongeBob's neighborhood weirdos meets Kung Fu Panda's Furious Five, if they all failed their fashion classes.

- Outcasts
- Differently abled
- Not society's idea of "divine"

But Shiva? He was like, "I see your inner awesome." He gave them purpose, power, and prime backstage passes to Mount Kailasa.

The Headless Incident: A Classic Case of "Even the greatest can lose control"

Parvati, home alone and needing a chill bath, tells her son: "Guard the door. No exceptions."

Kid takes his job more seriously than a Hufflepuff Prefect. Then comes Shiva. He's like, "Move." The boy's like, "Nope. DND. Talk to my hand."

Shiva's like, "Wrong answer," and... *slice*—there goes the head.

Yikes. Awkward.

Cue Divine Mom Rage

Parvati goes full Wanda Maximoff ballistic. Her fury shakes heaven and Earth. She tells Shiva: "Fix this, or else."

Shiva, realizing he messed up worse than SpongeBob in charge of the Krusty Krab, goes off to find a replacement head.

Plot Twist: Enter the Gana with the... Weird Head

One of the Ganas, brave and loyal like Cap himself, steps up. Offers his head. It wasn't your regular noggin either—some say it was... trunk-ish. Elephant-y, with a limb-like growth from the head.

Shiva, master of cosmic energy and interdimensional vibes, performs the first-ever ancient head transplant.

BOOM. Ganesha is born. Or more precisely, Gana-esha, Lord of the Ganas.

Wait — Was That the First Ever Head Transplant?!

Pause. This whole "head transplant" thing?

Modern scientists have *actually• explored this. No joke.

- Brain-dead donors
- Nerve reconnections
- Identity issues (because... new face?)
- Yogic healing potential (Shiva's ancient chakra skills, anyone?)

Yeah, myth perhaps, but if anyone had the know-how, it was Shiva, also potentially early sci-fi. Tony Stark would be intrigued.

So, that's the deal with the Elephant Head.

The Gana's head was already a little trunk-like. Or maybe storytellers picked elephants because:

- They are wise
- Strong but chill
- And Ganesha needed standout branding (hello, divine mascot!)

Or maybe folks just saw something they couldn't explain... and the ears and trunk got added in post-production.

Why This Story STILL Hits Hard

Ganesha's origin isn't just a myth—it's a multi-layered moral tale with:

- Forgiveness: Even beheading isn't the end of love.
- Inclusion: The "weirdos" save the day.
- Transformation: Tragedy becomes triumph.
- Hope: Even the worst mistake can be made right.

Final Thought: Not Just a Cute God with a Sweet Tooth

Ganesha isn't just here for your exams, modaks, and Instagram altars. He is a walking, blessing-giving reminder that:

- Everyone belongs—even if you feel like a rejected Avenger.
- Real power lies in kindness, wisdom, and self-awareness.
- What makes you "weird" might actually be your magic.

So next time you see Ganesha chilling with his snacks, remember:

He is more than lucky vibes. He is the divine CEO of second chances.

And honestly? We could all use a little Ganesha energy in our lives.

When Gana-Pathy becomes Gaja-Pathy.

Kuttichathan—The Mini-God with Max Attitude

Who is Kuttichathan?

Think Loki's mischief, Spider-Man's sense of justice, and Kung Fu Panda's flair—packed into one pint-sized legend.

In North Kerala (Malabar vibes!), there is chatter about this mini spirit with max energy. "Kutti" means child. "Chathan"? Spirit-ish. So: kid-spirit with chaos powers. Picture a dark-skinned boy with glowing red eyes, sky-riding bulls, and zero chill for injustice.

Demon? Nah. Anti-hero with a Heart? Absolutely.

Let's clear it up — Kuttichathan isn't your haunted mansion ghost or exorcism candidate. He is the folk hero who flips injustice on its head.

Origins: Born to Rebel

Back in the day:

- Temples had VIP-only signs
- Spiritual gates were locked for lower castes
- Power hoarders ran the show

So, who shows up? Not a prince, not a priest—but our guy, Kuttichathan. No golden throne—just backyard groves, smoky crossroads, and fierce vibes. If you were ignored, poor, or pushed down—he had your back.

Worship, Chathan Style

Forget gold crowns and epic chants. Kuttichathan is a "come as you are" god:

- Toddy? Yes.
- Cooked rice and meat? Absolutely.
- Oil lamps + good intentions? Now we're talking.

He even shows up through possession rituals. Think of it as a divine Zoom call—he drops in, shakes things up, and maybe borrows a snack.

What's the Takeaway?

Underneath the banana thefts and pot-shaking theatrics, Kuttichathan preaches:

- Stand up for the bullied—even if it's messy
- You don't need Sanskrit to be spiritual
- Mischief with a moral is sometimes holy
- Be barefoot, bold, and badass when needed

He's the god who shows up without warning—but always where justice is overdue. Basically, he is Kerala's undercover Avenger— with rice offerings instead of Stark tech.

The range of Kuttichathan's appearances (there have been some unverifiable run-ins with the demonic version in my own family!!)

Odiyan: Shadow Ninjas of Old Kerala

Whoa... Who Were the Odiyan?!

Imagine this: you are walking alone on a moonlit path in old-school Kerala when — BOOM! — someone leaps from the shadows, growls like a tiger, and vanishes like Batman with unfinished business.

Congrats. You just got Odiyan-ed.

Odiyan (plural: Odiyanmaar) were Kerala's stealth-mode shadow warriors—think Batman meets an Animagus.

The Sneaky Science Behind Odi Marachil

Forget Hogwarts-style dark magic. This was pure, tactical mischief. Back when landlords (jenmis) ruled like Thanos and the oppressed had no Avengers, Odiyanmaar fought back using:

- Black gear that blended with the night
- Animal disguises (serious cosplay cred)
- Terrifying growls
- Tree-leaping, shadow-hugging agility
- Night ops that belonged in a S.H.I.E.L.D. file

No gadgets. No CGI. Just fear turned into resistance—and sometimes, retaliation.

Myth Buster: Did They Really Shapeshift?

Let's be honest — if a dude in a buffalo mask jumped out under a full moon, you'd scream too. And your imagination did the rest. But, NO!! They didn't shapeshift.

Pre-Netflix Kerala didn't need special effects. Shadows were the drama.

How They Became Folklore Blockbusters

Folk songs (paattukathas) took these night missions and cranked them up to 11:

- "He drank oil and became a bull!"
- "He vanished into smoke!"
- " He shape-shifted mid-jump!"

Darkness + fear + poetic license = instant myth.

- Odiyan = Rebel, Not Villain
- No court. No clout. Seeking justice.
- No tweets. No speeches. Just shadow justice. His Mjölnir? Fear.

The Odiyan wasn't evil. He was clever, fed up, and fighting back.

Where the Odiyan Lives Today:

- On stage (Theyyam style)
- On screen (see Mohanlal's Odiyan)
- In sleepover stories that keep the lights on
- And in every underdog who fights back with wit, not weapons

Moral of the Story

Don't fear the mask.

Sometimes the quietest shadow carries the loudest message.

The Odiyan—using the cover of disguise and darkness to fight back

Yakshi — The Woman Who Said "Enough!"

Who Was the Yakshi?

Picture this: moonlit Kerala night, rustling leaves, eerie calm... and a woman with glowing eyes, red lips, and a quiet request for help.

Sounds like a ghost? Plot twist: she wasn't a spirit. She was a woman. Flesh, blood, and fury.

A Yakshi wasn't some phantom in white. She was someone who was cheated, violated, had loved, lost, and reached her breaking point. Not a monster — a woman the world pushed too far.

Not Evil. Just Enraged.

For generations, women, especially from marginalized communities, were wronged, silenced, and erased.

When justice failed, they didn't vanish. They transformed.

Yakshis were stories of rebellion, not horror. The original protesters. Kerala's ancient #MeToo.

Kaliyankaatu Neeli: The Comeback Queen

Meet Neeli — the Beyoncé of Yakshi lore.

- She was brilliant, brave, beautiful—and betrayed. But heartbreak didn't break her. It awakened her.
- She returned not to haunt, but to protect.
- Calling out cheaters, guarding the powerless, and flipping fear into justice.

Every "Revenge is Righteous" squad should have Neeli leading it.

From Forests to Temples

- Not all Yakshis stayed in the shadows.
- Some were worshipped—especially in Bhagavathy temples.
- Offered oil, flowers, and prayers—not to be feared but honored.

Because every wronged woman deserves more than pity—she deserves a pedestal.

Final Thought: Yakshis Were Never Demonic Vampires

- They weren't born in cemeteries.
- They were born in kitchens, fields, homes—until the world turned its back on them.
- Yakshis are Kerala's reminder that when justice sleeps, stories rise.

So, the next time someone mentions a Yakshi, don't flinch.

Think: Rebel. Survivor. Warrior in red. And maybe—offer her the respect she was always owed.

Good old Yakshi — she had to resort to scare tactics to survive. A little imagination to an already creative Malayali mind and BOOM! You can see how one can be scared out of their wits, especially the guilty!

Interlude 4:

Storytelling At The Dining Table
A Bridge To Rituals

Interlude 4: Storytelling at the Dining Table: A Bridge to Rituals

I basically grew up believing that every meal came with a free bonus feature — not a toy or a sticker, but a story. The kind that turned boring bites into blockbuster events. In our house, lunch wasn't lunch unless Valliamma launched into *the* Uncle tiger-and-Uncle fox tale. It didn't matter that I had heard it a hundred times. She told it with the same suspense as a season finale; the kind of delivery that made you lean in even when you already knew the twist. She had the storytelling energy of Po combined with the calm authority of a grandma who *knows* she's got you hooked.

And Amma had her own signature saga — the one about a boy who planted a tree on which unniyappams grew. Magical, fried, syrup-soaked unniyappams that could only exist in the delicious universe of Amma's stories. It was the kind of tale that made you chew slower just to stretch the moment.

Of course, some meals still called for magic. Like those nights when I absolutely refused a certain dish, and Amma had to summon her best weapon: the story of Adi paraashakti. A courtroom drama, no less — a man arguing with a king about whether it was a new moon (Amavasya) or a full moon. Everyone in the court knew the king was right. But the man, a stubborn devotee of Durga, wouldn't back down. So, the king gave him an ultimatum: prove the full moon appears on a new moon night, or face execution. Naturally, the man prays his heart out, the goddess answers, and boom — Pournami; miracle full moon. The king pardons him, and Amma, my very own goddess Durga, miraculously transformed my least favorite dinner into one I started *looking forward* to. That story became its own kind of lunar event — rare, brilliant, and capable of making me clean my plate.

Looking back, those stories weren't just entertainment. They were the soul of our meals, the soundtrack to my childhood. Every storyteller in my family had their signature move, their own narrative superpower.

Sure, my older cousins made fun of me for needing a full mythological feature film just to eat lunch but even they knew the ritual had power. They'd hang around for the retellings, laughing and listening, even if they pretended it was just background noise.

Those stories shaped how I see the world. They made food taste better, memories stick harder, and everyday moments feel like magic. I used to think Hogwarts was the only place with spells but turns out, the real magic was already at the table, hiding inside every bite, whispered between spoonfuls, and told by people who didn't need wands to cast them.

But unlike Valliamma and Amma, I didn't have to bring out my full myth-weaving toolkit every time I fed my children. By then, Disney and Nickelodeon had cracked the code—bite-sized cartoon episodes that ran just long enough to get through a meal. With *Barney*, *SpongeBob*, or *Dora the Explorer* running in the background, every lunch became less of an epic battle and more of a co-op level with built-in entertainment. I still dropped in the occasional story, sure but thankfully, I didn't have to carry the whole plot on my back like a one-man Avengers team.

That gift — to tell, to listen, to imagine, and to believe in stories clearly passed down the family tree. Years later, my toddler daughter watched me plant a maple sapling in our backyard and, with absolute conviction, named it the chalupa tree. She truly believed it would someday grow actual Taco Bell chalupas. And honestly, the name stuck. We still call that now-giant maple the chalupa tree. A perfect mash-up of fairy-tale imagination and toddler taste buds, inspired by her ride-or-die food loves back then: chalupas and chicken nuggets.

CHAPTER 13B:
Traditions We Put Up With:
THE SACRED, THE SILLY & THE SERIOUSLY UNDERRATED

Chapter 13 B: The Traditions We Put Up With—The Sacred, the Silly, and the Seriously Underrated

Here's where we finally answer life's big questions like:

- Why is there a coconut on my textbook?
- Who decided turmeric could fix everything?
- And why do we suddenly wake up at 4 a.m. to boil rice and chant during full moons?

Well, not exactly the above—but here is the deal: Hindu traditions are not just ancient—they are efficient, meaningful, and often just the right amount of mysterious. They help us mark time, honor our people, reset with the seasons, and occasionally confuse house guests.

This chapter is your backstage pass to it all. Think of it as:

"The Dharma Is in the Details" — Hogwarts-worthy habits your grandma swears by, and Kung Fu Panda-grade discipline hidden in your daily routines.

In Kerala's Hindu homes, tradition isn't something you learn from a textbook—it is something you live.

From lighting a lamp at dusk to walking barefoot to a temple, these everyday actions connect the ordinary with the divine. They aren't just about being religious, they are about remembering who we are, where we come from, and what we value. Passed down through generations, these rituals shape identity, bring families together, and quietly teach us discipline, gratitude, and respect.

In this chapter, we explore the customs that make up the rhythm of daily life and how they continue to guide and ground a new generation. Let's go full Doctor Strange and look into the multiverse of meaning in our most underrated household habits.

📜 Sandhyavandanam: The Original Mindfulness Routine

(Long Before You Paid for Meditation Apps)

Sandhyavandanam might sound like it came straight out of Professor Dumbledore's curriculum but trust me, it is one of the OG spiritual hacks.

At its heart, this ancient ritual is all about staying in sync with nature and carving out quiet moments to reconnect with your inner self; kind of like your soul's version of a morning scroll, minus the doom.

Traditionally done three times a day —sunrise, noon, and sunset— it's like your own personal Hogwarts timetable, with mantras instead of magic spells and sun salutations instead of spellcasting.

Here is what it usually includes (think of it as your spiritual Avengers warm-up):

- Achamana — Sipping water while chanting mantras to purify your system. Basically, hydration meets intention.
- Pranayama — Deep breathing to calm your mind. Master Shifu-approved breath control right here.

- Arghya-dana — Offering water to the rising or setting sun, which is basically you saying, "What's up?" to the cosmic Wi-Fi.
- Chanting the Gayatri Mantra — Like launching your mental Jarvis system. It is a powerful, time-tested code for clarity and wisdom.

Originally reserved for the twice-born (dvija) castes (another Brahminic twist), the deeper goal of Sandhyavandanam was never about gatekeeping. It is about mindfulness, gratitude, and clearing mental clutter.

In many Kerala homes today, it has morphed into simpler rituals: lighting a lamp at twilight, whispering prayers, and soaking in a few sacred moments. No subscriptions. No fancy mats. Just you, some peace, and a breath away from universal alignment.

So yeah, turns out your grandma was doing mindful breathing and cosmic syncing before it became an app trend. Respect.

🪔 Lighting the Nilavilakku: The Lamp That Ended Playtime and Started Your Existential Crisis

If you have grown up in a Kerala home, you have probably seen the Nilavilakku — the tall, graceful brass lamp — glowing softly in the corner of the pooja room or hallway. It is usually lit twice a day, at dawn and dusk, to welcome light, positivity, and divine presence into the home. But for many of us, it was more than just a religious ritual; it was a part of daily life we couldn't ignore... even if we tried.

I still remember how it went down at Valliamma's illam. We'd be in the middle of an intense game — mostly the infamous L O N D O N in the open courtyard or carrom board game with my younger brothers and cousins — completely absorbed and unaware of time. Then out of nowhere, one of my aunts, or Kunhimalu or Devaki Amma (the domestic helpers), would appear with the lit lamp in hand, chanting softly, "Deepam... Deepam..."

And just like that everything stopped. No matter how close we were to winning or losing the game, we dropped everything, stood still, and joined in reciting the shloka:

🔱 शिवं भवतु कल्याणं, आयुरारोग्य वर्दनं।

मम: शत्रुविनाशाय, दीपज्वालायते नम:॥

"May this lamp bring peace, health, and long life; I bow to the flame that destroys both inner and outer enemies."

It might have been negotiable, but importantly, it was a habit that we all enjoyed being a part of, in some weird way. As kids, though, it meant one thing: playtime was over. It was our daily reminder that homework was waiting, and so was reality. The lights at home would be turned on only after this ritual.

But looking back now, I realize the ritual had layers we didn't see at the time. Lighting the Nilavilakku isn't about religion. It is about creating a pause, about marking the transition — from chaos to calm, from activity to awareness.

The lamp's flame represents knowledge. The wick is your ego. The oil is your desires. When the flame burns, it slowly consumes both, leaving behind only clarity.

So next time you see a lamp being lit at home or in a temple, pause. Channel your inner Master Shifu. Imagine Dumbledore whispering, "Lumos." Picture Tony Stark tinkering with the Arc Reactor of your soul.

It might just be the universe reminding you to turn on your inner light.

💬 Dedication: A special shout-out to everyone who has ever paused or lost a game because someone whispered "Deepam..." when you were totally locked in — like Thor mid-hammer swing.

Footnote to the tradition of lighting lamps:

🪔 First, Light the Lamp. Then Everything Else.

When my son was a toddler, he had one non-negotiable spiritual routine on his India visits: his grandma had to light a lamp. Often. For absolutely no reason. He'd tug at her hand, march her to the pooja room, and insist on the ritual. No special festival, no chant — just the joy of watching a flickering flame come alive. Amma named it "Kunju-mon's lamp"—the Li'l Kid's Lamp.

That toddler-level awe? Honestly, it's spot on.

Because if there's one ritual beloved across Hindu homes and temples, it is lighting the lamp.

Whether it is a majestic brass deepam tall enough to need scaffolding or a humble steel diya tucked beside your spice rack, this is where it all begins. Always.

Why?

Because in Hindu thought, light isn't just light.

It is awareness.

It is presence.

It is the quiet removal of darkness — literal, metaphorical, and occasionally emotional (especially during power cuts and midlife crises).

Lighting a lamp is more than routine. It is a reset button. A sacred spark that brings clarity to confusion, order to chaos, and a sense of intention to your day. A philosophical mic drop, disguised as flame.

🌱 Tulasi: Holy Basil, Batman!

The Plant That's a Goddess, Mosquito Repellent, and Life Coach

If you've ever walked into a traditional Kerala home, you might have noticed a special little structure in the courtyard or by the front door, with a plant growing on top. That's the Tulasi thara—home to the sacred Tulasi plant, also known as Holy Basil.

But this isn't just any plant. In Hindu homes, Tulasi is treated like a living goddess; strong, radiant, and full of protective energy.

Every day, someone in the house —often a grandmother, a parent, or even a mini wizard-in-training (a.k.a. a child)— waters the Tulasi. In the evening, a small oil lamp is lit nearby, and sometimes people walk around it (pradakshina) offering prayers and asking for blessings.

But Tulasi isn't just sitting there being holy and photogenic. It is also a legit multitasker:

- Natural mosquito repellent (Voldemort to dengue)
- Air purifier (Iron Man-level tech in leaf form)
- Sacred, symbolic, and scientifically smart

Long before bug sprays and those zappy mosquito rackets that make you feel like Thor with a tennis racket, Tulasi kept things fresh, clean, and bite-free.

So next time you see a Tulasi plant glowing under a soft lamp, remember:

It is not just a plant. It's your home's miniature Groot— calm, centered, and silently saving your ecosystem one leaf at a time.

Face Marks with Meaning: What's That on Your Forehead? And Why It's Cooler Than a Tattoo

Ever looked at someone and thought, "Why do they have white lines, a red dot, or something yellowish on their forehead?" Welcome to the world of spiritual stickers—also known as vibhuti, kumkum, and chandanam.

These aren't fashion statements (though they're totally aesthetic). They are ancient symbols that carry deep meaning and purpose. Let's break it down like we're in the Room of Requirement:

- 🕉️ Vibhuti (Sacred Ash):

    This gray-white ash is usually smeared across the forehead in three horizontal lines — like spiritual war paint for Lord Shiva fans. It is a bold reminder that everything in life, including our worries and our egos, eventually turns to ash. In short: stay humble, stay grounded. Hulk-level smash on the ego.

- 🔴 **Kumkum (Vermilion Red Powder):**

  That little red dot — nope, it is not from a sticker pack — it is kumkum, often worn at the center of the forehead, right between the eyebrows (a.k.a. the ajna chakra or third eye spot). It represents Shakti, or the divine feminine energy. Think of it as a cosmic Wi-Fi hotspot for focus, intuition, and inner strength.

- 🟡 **Chandanam (Sandalwood Paste):**

  This cool, yellowish paste is basically the original chill pill. It soothes the body and mind and is often applied during temple visits. It smells amazing, too. Symbolically, it stands for devotion, calmness, and peaceful vibes. Po would 100% approve.

Apart from being deeply personal, these markings also tell a story about what traditions your family follows, what deity you feel connected to, or what kind of spiritual energy you are trying to channel for the day.

So, the next time you see someone with a forehead mark, know this: it's not just a dot, a line, or a dab. It's a quiet badge of faith, a forehead-level reminder to stay mindful, and honestly… a pretty cool connection to thousands of years of tradition.

Whether you are casting spells or smashing bad guys, this mark? It is your daily dose of spiritual style.

vibhuti   kumkum   chandanam

🍛 Naivedyam: "The First Dosa Goes to God"

(Even If Amma Made It and You Are the Oldest, Hungriest, and Hates Sharing Food)

Imagine you have just cooked something amazing—hot, steamy rice, maybe a crispy dosa, or the kind of sambar that makes your soul happy. You are about to take that glorious first bite when your grandma says:

"Keep that aside for God!"

Wait, what? God gets the first bite? You made it! You didn't even burn it this time!

Welcome to the tradition of Naivedyam — the sacred habit of offering the first dish of the day to the divine (and sometimes to the ancestors too). It is like giving your cosmic guest a taste before the rest of the squad digs in.

But Why Though?

Well, in Hindu tradition, it is believed that when you offer the first portion of food to a deity or to your ancestors (especially your mom's side — because we all know grandma doesn't mess around), you are showing gratitude and respect.

You are saying:

"Hey, thanks for the food, the family, and not letting that curry explode while I was distracted by reels."

It is also believed that your ancestors still look out for you—sort of like spiritual grandparents keeping an eye on your homework and your snack choices from the other side.

The OG Plot Twist: The Sage and the Selfless Woman

There is an old story about a poor woman who had just enough food for herself. She was super hungry but when a wandering sage spoiler alert: he was a god in disguise (or as I'd like to think, a saint and not some supernatural being descended from a portal door that Dr. Strange just opened up for the heck of it) showed up at her door, she gave him her only meal.

He blessed her, and abundance, joy, and probably unlimited ladoos followed.

The moral?

Selflessness > selfishness. Also, you never know when the hungry guy knocking is some cleverly disguised deva testing your hospitality game. (Totally a Dr. Strange move.)

What's the Lesson Here (Besides Sharing is Caring)? This tradition isn't about feeding invisible guests. It is about remembering:

- Gratitude for what you have
- Respect for where you come from
- Generosity, even when it's hard
- And the idea that when you give first, you are growing more, not losing anything

So yeah, maybe your dosa is going cold but your karma is heating up.

🏠The Kanni Moola: Where Your House Has a Vibe Manager

In every good old Kerala home, there is this mysterious southwest corner called the Kanni Moola. And no, it is not where the Wi-Fi dies or where your missing socks go — it is way cooler (and spookier).

Every day, someone (usually grandma, the unsung spiritual superhero) lights a lamp there. Why? Because, according to tradition, that corner is basically VIP real estate for friendly house spirits.

Yup, your house has roommates — invisible, low-maintenance ones who don't hog the bathroom but will protect your place from evil, floods, bad vibes, and maybe even terrible relatives.

Legend says:

Homes that kept their Kanni Moola spirits happy? Totally disaster-proof. Think Avengers-level defense mode.

Homes that skipped the ritual? Let's just say... the roof didn't always stay where it should.

So, lighting that lamp each day?

- It is not just tradition
- it is spiritual antivirus software.

Think of it as hitting "update and protect" on your house's energy system, with ghee and a cotton wick.

Moral of the story:

Respect the corner. Light the lamp. And if you feel an oddly good vibe in the room? That's just your invisible home buddy giving you a nod of approval—like Dumbledore twinkling from behind his half-moon specs.

Menstruation and Temple Rules: Periods, Purity, and the Temple Ban

Respectfully Calling Out the Cosmic Double Standard

Ah yes, the ancient debate: "She is on her period—should she enter the temple, or just binge-watch Netflix with a hot water bottle?" Let's talk about it. With humor. And honesty.

In many traditional Hindu households—including in Kerala—menstruation has been labeled "ritually impure." That's right, a totally normal biological function gets the same treatment as muddy shoes on a white bedsheet.

Suddenly, when you are on your period:

- Temples are off-limits
- Poojas are a no-go
- Kitchens might as well have "AUTHORIZED PERSONNEL ONLY" signs
- And grandma's radar is more accurate than any period tracker app

Where Did This Come From?

These ideas come from old-school notions of shuddhi (purity) and ashuddhi (impurity)—back when people didn't have Google, Advil, or a clue about uterine biology. The logic? Menstruation = body in "cleansing mode," so stay spiritually lowkey for a few days.

Sounds poetic. But also... a little outdated, no? Even Master Shifu would raise an eyebrow.

The Great Plot Twist: Not All Traditions Agree

Before you roll your eyes and light a feminist fire, here's a twist: not all Hindu traditions see menstruation as impure.

In Assam, during the Ambubachi Mela, they literally celebrate a goddess's period. Yup, Mother Earth herself takes time off—no temple rituals, just rest and reverence.

Let us not forget:

- Some goddesses are believed to menstruate.
- Some cultures worship the shakti (power) in menstruation.
- Some families are chill, handing you a heat pad and a ladle to stir the sambar.

So... What Now?

The truth? It's complicated.

Some still follow the "no temple during periods" rule. Others toss it aside like an old instruction manual written in Sanskrit.

What's important is this:

Menstruation is not a flaw. It is not dirty. It is not a spiritual glitch. It is power. It is biology. And it is yours.

Spiritual Mic Drop:

You can respect traditions and question them. You can honor rituals and ask for better logic.

As for the divine? Pretty sure she's not afraid of a menstrual cycle. Especially when she created it.

🧭 FIELD GUIDE: Everyday Rituals in Kerala's Hindu Homes

🧘 Sandhyavandanam — The OG mindfulness app
Daily sun salutes, mantra chanting, and breathwork = the soul's version of a morning scroll.

🪔 Lighting the Nilavilakku — Your inner light switch
Flame = knowledge. Wick = ego. Oil = desires. Dumbledore vibes at dusk.

🌿 Tulasi Plant Worship — Groot meets Goddess
Mosquito-fighting, air-purifying spiritual legend rooted in your courtyard.

🛡️ Forehead Marks — Symbolic skin-level superpowers
Ash = humility | Kumkum = divine energy | Sandalwood = calm mode activated.

🍚 Naivedyam — "God gets first dibs" rule
Offering the first bite to the divine = spiritual gratitude + secret abundance cheat code.

🏠 Kanni Moola — Your home's spiritual firewall
Daily lamp lighting = antivirus + good vibes update for the house.

🩸 Periods and Purity—Questioning the tradition
No temple rule ≠ cosmic truth. Menstruation = power, not impurity. #ShaktiAwakens

INTERLUDE 5: MENSTRUAL MAYHEM AND THE GREAT UNDERWEAR RESCUE OPERATION

I was probably all of 6 or 7. One of my aunts was on her period. The house rules? Totally, Hogwarts-level strange.

Rule: She had to eat separately. No one could touch her. Especially kids. If a kid *did* touch her, she had full license to grab said child and not let go until someone brought them new clothes.

How new clothes came into this spiritual quarantine clause is more bizarre than expecting Po to have a six-pack by summer. But again, being who I was (read: a certified trouble magnet), I had to find out. Curiosity, meet chaos.

So, I touched her. On purpose.

And she GRABBED me like a Dementor looking for a soul snack. I fought like she was the Yakshi come to drink my blood. I screamed. I wailed. I tried every Avengers move I knew—including the Black Widow elbow twist and the Hulk scream.

And guess what? Nobody batted an eyelid.

Some of my older cousins even *giggled*. (Probably took bets on how long I'd last.)

So Valliamma, in all her "let's fix this fast" wisdom, sent Raghavan to get me new clothes. Because, of course, nothing solves magical-period contamination like a fresh set of undies and a cartoon t-shirt.

After a good 20 minutes of imprisonment by this menstrual Yakshi, I was finally released from her iron grip.

And that, my friends, was my first hands-on lesson in bodily autonomy, social taboos, and never messing with tradition unless you've got a spare outfit ready.

(Side note: My Aunt got a hero's welcome. Me? I got a lecture and a lime juice. Totally worth it.)

Section 5:

Power Moves
—From Nature to Nirvana

CHAPTER 14
SEASONAL RITES
WHEN NATURE TELLS US WHAT TO CELEBRATE

Chapter 14: Seasonal Rites— When Nature Tells Us What to Celebrate 🌦️ ✨

Welcome to Kerala's Festival Multiverse— where Mother Nature calls the shots, astrology does the event planning, and your grandma is not only the head chef but also the unofficial life coach, spiritual DJ, and pappadam-quality control officer. Whether you are fasting like Doctor Strange during a mystical cleanse, detoxing like Po in training montage mode, or just hoping you don't burn your mundu while lighting a Vishu lamp, consider this your user manual for Dharma done right (and with some flair).

Nature's Calendar: Mother Earth Is the Real CEO

You think school timetables or your favorite show's drop dates matter? Ha. In Kerala, seasons are the boss, and every coconut tree knows it.

I. 🌧️ Monsoon = Cleanse Mode Activated!

When the rain clouds roll in like a moody Bollywood hero and the streets turn into slip-n-slide zones, it's time to slow down and soul up. Think of it as a spiritual software update:

Ramayana Readathon—

Families gather to binge on this ancient epic as if it's the latest Netflix miniseries. Bonus: It comes with built-in life lessons and no cliffhangers.

Q: But why Ramayana? Why not read Mahabharata or the Gita?

A: Monsoon = Mood for Myths

Just like how you wouldn't start Avengers: Endgame on a random Tuesday but save it for prime time feels, Ramayana is that perfect monsoon binge.

1. Ramayana = Hero's Journey Vibes

Think: Harry Potter Book 1. It's a clean, feel-good, origin story with big dharma energy. Less grey area, more straight-up right vs wrong. Monsoons need clarity, not chaos.

2. Mahabharata = Emotional Rollercoaster

It's like Infinity War — intense, layered, too many characters dying or lying. Save it for winter or exam season when your brain is ready for moral debates and drama.

3. Bhagavad Gita = Inner Work, Not Outer Vibes

It's like Dumbledore giving Harry life lectures — powerful but needs full attention and a dry weather brain. Gita is peak philosophy mode, not exactly rainy-day chill.

TL; DR:

Ramayana hits different when it's pouring outside—heroes, forests, love, exile, epic rescues. It's the OG monsoon saga

🛕 Temple Talks—

The OG TED Talks (a.k.a. discourses, pravachans, or spiritual satsangs), only way older, with sacred chants 🎶 instead of keynotes, and the smell of sandalwood replacing overpriced lattes.

Q: Why are Temple Talks held in the monsoon season though?

A: Here goes ...

1. It's Pause Season IRL

During monsoon, farmers pause ploughing, travel slows down, and nature hits refresh. So, humans go:

"If we can't hustle outside, let's level up inside."

2. Perfect Mood for Mythology

Rain outside + stories inside = ultimate vibe. It's like binge-watching Loki but with dharma lessons. The Ramayan, Bhagavatam, etc., get narrated in cozy temple halls. No FOMO. Only JOMO + Monsoon.

3. Tradition Meets Chill Season

Our rishis were smart: they used Chaturmas (a 4-month holy period) for teaching and tuning in. Monsoon = fewer distractions = more likely you'll actually listen and not scroll halfway through.

4. Vibe Check: High

Monsoon is romantic and reflective. So is temple talk. Imagine Gandalf dropping life wisdom but in Sanskrit and with prasadam after.

TL; DR:

Temple Talks during monsoon = spiritual TED Talks in nature's cozy blanket. You slow down, sit down, and glow up.

🍲 Karkidaka Kanji—

Grandma's sacred power soup. It tastes like boiled wisdom, is spicier than your love life, and heals everything from tummy tantrums to existential dread.

🌧 Monsoon = Mood. Cleanse your home, your body, your karma.

No rain, no gain.

Q: If Kanji is that good, then why not year-round? What is so special about the monsoon season? Monsoon sounds like perfect biriyani weather to me

A: Because

1. Karkidakam = Kerala's "Reset Month"

It's like the July Hogwarts break—no new projects, no weddings, just chill, reflect, detox. So, the food goes soft, warm, and healing—enter Kanji (rice porridge). Think of it as Kerala's soul soup.

2. Body's Tired, Gut's Moody

Monsoon messes with digestion. So, Ayurveda says:

"Yo, skip the biriyani. Go light, go warm, go Kanji."

It's the green smoothie of ancient Kerala — only it's made of rice, cumin, garlic, and love.

3. Grandma-Level Wizardry

Your grandma's medicinal Kanji is like Snape's potion, minus the bitterness. She adds special herbs (jeerakam, muthari, ulluva, and dashapushpam) for full-body balance.

4. Karkidakam = Also, the Spiritual Season

We're reading Ramayanam, doing temple talks, and detoxing our karma. So, the food has to match. Simple, sattvic, sacred. Kanji = edible meditation.

TL; DR:

Kanji in Karkida = Kerala's comfort potion for mind, body, and monsoon mood.

Like ramen in winter or hot cocoa at Hogwarts—only with more cumin.

✔ Shivothi—Kerala's OG Cleaning Day!

Hey fam, ever heard of Shivothi? It's the Hindu version of Clean-Up Day that our grandparents took seriously. Happened every year in Kerala on the last day of Midhunam (that's mid-July-ish), right before the monsoon-y Karkidakam vibes kicked in.

What did people do?

Not yoga, not reels, not even a beach clean-up. They literally scrubbed every dusty corner, torched old junk and then placed a symbol of Goddess Bhagavathi (happy mom vibes) in the prayer room to chill with her for the month.

Now we've got Earth Day, Yoga Day, Dog Day, Avocado Day... but we forgot our own ancestral "Detox Day". And guess what? Swachh Bharat is cool, but Shivothi did it before it was cool.

It's not just about brooms and bleach. It is about cleaning your space and your spirit. Time to revive this desi deep-clean tradition — and maybe clean out that closet you've been ignoring since 2022.

Let us bring Shivothi back. For the house. For our health. For good vibes only. ♻️,

II. Cosmic Checkpoints: Ritual DLCs

In the Sanatana Dharma universe, every moon phase unlocks a new quest. Consider these your limited-time spiritual events. No loot boxes, just pure vibes.

🎉 Utsavams—The Ultimate Temple Turn-Ups

Imagine if Hogwarts, Coachella, and an ancient Sanskrit saga had a baby.

- Elephants in full armor (yes, real ones—sorry, no CGI here)
- Fireworks lighting up the sky like it's a Desi Marvel crossover
- Chariot parades that make Fast and Furious look like a tricycle race
- Priests chanting like they are casting spells and uncles dancing like they are possessed by rhythm itself

This isn't just a ritual. It is a cosmic party with a guest list that includes deities, ancestors, and your second cousin with the unbeatable Thiruvathira moves.

🌑 Spiritual Boss Levels—Ekadashi, Amavasya, Pournami, Shivaratri

These days are like those final levels in video games: fewer distractions, higher stakes.

- No rice (detox mode)
- No reels (introspection mode)

- Lamps lit as if your inner light has been sponsored by the Sun God ☀️
- Chants so powerful even Yoda would stop mid-meditation to listen 🧘‍♂️🐚

You versus Your Ego—fight night, celestial edition.

🕊️ Karkidaka Vavu Bali—Ancestral Uber Eats

Once a year, Keralites send rice-ball tributes to their ancestors. It is like a sacred DoorDash delivery to the beyond—except wetter and with more chanting.

Imagine if Hogwarts had a "Send Food to Ghosts" day. Now add banana leaves, riverside rituals, and silent respect. That is Vavu Bali.

Not scary, just sacred. And slightly soggy.

III. Festival 2.0: Dharma Meets Wi-Fi

Because who says rituals can't trend on TikTok?

Onam in NYC, Vishu in Dubai—The Diaspora Diaries

Malayalis are like coconut oil: everywhere. So are their festivals.

- Zoom-poojas with buffering priests
- Payasam mailed in Tupperware like edible love letters
- Aunties forwarding 100 Vishu memes before breakfast
- Global pookkalam competitions with hashtags like #FloralFlex

Kerala may be small, but its festivals? Borderless.

Eco Is the New Epic—Dharma Goes Green

Forget plastic deities and chemical crackers. This generation is rewriting rituals with Earth in mind.

- Turmeric idols = compostable, biodegradable, bless-able
- Solar lamps at temples = sustainable sparkle
- Banana leaf > plastic plate. Always.

The new dharma? Save the Earth like it is your grandma's sari collection: precious, delicate, and way more powerful than it looks.

🤸 Young Dharma Defenders—Culture Has a Comeback Crew

There's a whole millennial squad reviving old-school cool.

- Learning Thiruvathira with YouTube tutorials
- Rocking mundus at Pooram like its fashion week
- Organizing temple clean-ups with more coordination than group projects

These aren't "just traditions." They are our superpowers in slow-motion.

The Eternal Vibe: Dharma Never Dies

You might be posting your Vishu lamp on Insta, silently folding your palms for your ancestors, or dancing in the rain with a kanji hangover—whatever your ritual, it counts.

Here's the golden takeaway for your inner Dharma Dashboard:

- Celebrate with purpose
- Align with nature
- Live your Dharma—especially when no one is watching

Because the real flex? Knowing you belong to a culture where even rain has rituals and even silence is sacred. As SpongeBob once probably said,

"I'm ready... for inner peace."

Seasonal Rites Field Guide

A quick-look emoji-powered cheat sheet to Kerala's seasonal festivals, spiritual rituals, and culture with a cosmic twist.

☂️**Monsoon Detox Season**

Ramayana readings, temple talks, deep-clean your home and headspace, and healing porridge (Karkidaka Kanji).

🎉 **Utsavams**

Temple festivals synced with the stars—complete with elephants and fireworks.

🕉️ **Power Days**

Ekadashi, Amavasya, Pournami, and Shivaratri = fasting, prayers, spiritual energy.

🌊 **Karkidaka Vavu Bali**

Annual ancestor ritual with rice balls and blessings by the river.

✈️**Onam Abroad**

Global Malayalis are throwing traditional parties in high-rise apartments.

📸 **Vishu Livestream**

Digital Vishukkani, real blessings, and cash-filled cultural unboxings.

♻️ **Eco-Friendly Celebrations**

Clay Ganeshas, low-smoke Vishu, and grandma-approved flower power.

🕵️ **Forgotten Festivals Revival**

Youngsters rediscovering Pooram, Thiruvathira, and more with a techy flair.

🌏**Core Festival Vibe**

Gratitude, harmony, and dharma that evolve with the times.

CHAPTER 15:

From Payasam to Pyrotechnics
Kerala's Festival State of Mind

Chapter 15: From Payasam to Pyrotechnics—Kerala's Festival State of Mind

🎉 Part 1—The Vibe: Why Festivals Matter

Let's be honest—festivals in Kerala are the closest thing to a real-life mash-up of Hogwarts magic, an Avengers Endgame event, and Kung Fu Panda's spiritual energy — plus SpongeBob-level excitement.

You have got:

- Sadyas (feasts that rival any Hogwarts Great Hall dinner)
- Pookkalams (flower carpets prettier than Professor Sprout's greenhouse)
- Boat races (fast, furious, and river-bending like an Avatar water tribe match)
- Firecrackers that make Hulk nervous, and Iron Man suit up
- Drums that could summon Thor

But beneath the sparkle and chaos lies purpose. In Sanatana Dharma, festivals aren't random public holidays. They are seasonal, lunar, and cosmic calendar syncs that hit refresh on your soul.

Think of them as universe-approved pause buttons with built-in lessons on gratitude, community, and dharma.

Why it still matters:

- Hit pause on the hustle and your screen addiction
- Be grateful—even for that cousin who photobombs everything.
- Reconnect—with your family, nature, ancestors, and the Wi-Fi of the cosmos
- Celebrate values like kindness, discipline, balance, and truth

So yeah, maybe you came for the banana chips and kaineettam (usually money)—but you stayed for the spiritual Wi-Fi and emotional upgrade.

📅 **Kerala Festival Cheat Sheet:**

- January—Temple Utsavams (drums, fire, processions—true community theater)
- March/April—Vishu (solar new year; prosperity focus)
- July—Karkidakam (Ramayana month, healing food, and introspection)
- August/September—Onam (harvest + Mahabali's symbolic homecoming)
- September/October—Navaratri (Goddess + wisdom season)
- February/March—Attukal Pongala (women-led devotion with fire and payasam)
- Various—Shivaratri, Ekadashi, and temple-specific utsavams

🔥 Part 2—The Big 4 (And One Mega Bonus)

Onam—The Festival That Outsmarts the Gods (Literally)

Every year, Kerala explodes into celebration: pookkalams, sadyas, boat races, banana chip flexing. But at the heart is a story about King Mahabali — a ruler so beloved, he got booted underground.

Let's revisit that legend. Mahabali, the people's king, had everything: prosperity, peace, and popularity. The gods? Not thrilled. So, Vishnu shape-shifted into a tiny Brahmin and pulled off the classic underdog-to-giant flex, demanding "three paces of land" and sending Mahabali to the underworld.

Sounds suspiciously like a godly ego problem, not a Mahabali one.

Spoiler alert:

He was punished not for arrogance, but for being too competent without being part of the elite priestly club. Brahmin 🙄

But here's the Kerala twist — we don't weep for Mahabali. We welcome him.

We flip the narrative:

- Pookkalams that would earn Professor Sprout's full marks
- Boat races that rival Wakandan water battles
- Sadyas, where each banana leaf is a culinary scroll of flavor

Onam is a rebellion wrapped in a smile. It's harvest pride, egalitarian memory, and festive defiance—disguised as florals and food.

Vishu — Reset for the Soul

Vishu is that magical reset button we all wish we had. New year, new vibe. You wake up, and the first thing you see is the Vishukkani—fruits, gold, flowers, lamps, and a perfectly placed cucumber that's somehow holier than your alarm clock.

Your mom? She has been channeling her inner Wong all night, arranging everything just right so that when you open your eyes, the universe says: "Welcome. Let us try again."

Then comes:

- Firecrackers—because nothing says renewal like dodging explosions
- Kaineettam—cash from elders with the energy of Tony Stark funding your dreams
- Sadya—because you deserve another feast after surviving the fiscal year

Forget destiny resets—this is a mood reset. Vishu isn't about fate; it is about focus. Start fresh. Dream big. And don't burn your eyebrows.

📚 Navaratri—Bookworms Assemble

In Kerala, Navaratri isn't a battle scene—it is a quiet salute to knowledge.

While other states celebrate demon-slaying Durga, we go full Hermione Granger.

Enter Ayudha Pooja, the one day when your textbooks, laptops, violins, and calculators get treated better than you.

Everything that helps you learn or create is cleaned, worshipped, and honored. Saraswati takes center stage. Your homework? Sent on paid leave.

Then comes Vijayadashami:

- Toddlers trace the first letters in rice (the sacred keyboard).
- Students pray for less buffering in the brain.
- Tools of the trade get divine upgrades.

It is a festival where silence speaks louder than shlokas, and learning is the highest form of worship.

🥣 Attukal Pongala—Smoke, Sisterhood, and Sacred Calories

Trivandrum transforms into the largest open-air temple kitchen on the planet.

The roads shut down. The city listens. And women of all ages light fires, cook Pongala, and form an invisible net of divine energy stronger than the Sorcerer Supreme's shield.

The ingredients? Jaggery, banana, rice, coconut. The vibe? Strength, unity, devotion.

No influencers. No hashtags. Just sweat, fire, and unshakable faith.

Pro Tips:

- Bring shade. Umbrellas are holy gear.
- Hydrate like you are preparing for a fire-bending duel.
- Come for the Pongala, stay for the matriarchal power surge.

🐦 Thrissur Pooram—When Divinity Drops the Bass

If Hogwarts and Wakanda had a festival baby and raised it in Kerala, it'd be Thrissur Pooram.

It is loud, bold, and utterly brilliant.

- Kudamattam: synchronized umbrella-switching battles atop elephants
- Ilanjithara Melam: a percussion symphony so powerful, Hulk would dance
- Fireworks: Not your average Diwali—this is cosmic-level pyrotechnics

THRISSUR POORAM

Originally started by Shakthan Thampuran to unite all communities, Thrissur Pooram is where tradition, rebellion, and rhythm collide. And now it unites the galaxy (almost). Come for the percussion, stay for the spiritual bass drop.

If Kerala had to nominate one festival to represent it on a cosmic catwalk, it would be Thrissur Pooram. It is a divine flex, percussion showdown, fireworks face-off, and royal elephant parade—rolled into one.

Held at the Vadakkunnathan Temple, this isn't a dusty relic—it is alive, loud, and pulsing with power.

It is divinity in full volume, zero gatekeeping. Consider this your golden ticket.

*About elephants —Tradition or Trauma?

When Culture Crosses the Line—and the Line Tramples Back

Let us talk about the massive elephant in the room. Literally. Elephants in festivals like Thrissur Pooram may look majestic under golden headdresses and parasols, but let's be honest—this isn't tradition, it's trauma in costume.

These gentle giants are paraded through blazing heat, bursting fireworks, and ear-splitting crowds, all while chained, poked, and made to "perform."

Over the last decade, Kerala alone has witnessed over 600 incidents where distressed elephants have panicked, run amok, or tragically injured themselves and others. And who gets blamed? The elephant, of course.

They lose their dignity, freedom, and often their sanity. They get beaten, starved, or exiled into lonely captivity—because we refuse to read the clear signs of distress on a 4,000-kg creature trapped in a sea of fireworks and fanfare.

Here's the truth: tradition evolves.

We gave up child marriage and animal sacrifices. It's time we gave up this, too.

No god asked for suffering in the name of celebration. Let us rewrite the playbook—this time with compassion, not chains.

IF WE REVERE ELEPHANTS AS GANESHA'S KIN...
ISN'T IT TIME WE LET THEM LIVE LIKE IT?

🌿 Part 3—The Meaning: Keep It Real, Keep It Rooted

Kerala's festivals aren't just about colors and carbs.

They are:

- Rooted in the Earth
- Aligned with the stars
- Written in ancient scripts and sung by your grandma

Today, you might see Onam reels on Instagram and livestream Pongala—but that doesn't make it less sacred.

Next time your parents say, "Come help with the pookkalam" or "Go light the lamp"—don't roll your eyes. Suit up.

Be the Peter Parker. Be the Hermione. Because Kerala's festivals? They're not just celebrations.

They are sacred side quests.

Field Guide: Festival Fever in a Flash

Here's your cheat sheet to Kerala's festival frenzy. Packed with vibes, values, and just enough emojis to make your grandma curious.

Festival	Emoji Vibe	Theme	Core Values	Why Gen Z Should Care
Onam		Harvest & Homecoming	Gratitude, Community, Tradition	Big feast, big vibes, and Mahabali's comeback story
Vishu		Solar New Year	Renewal, Hope, Prosperity	Cultural Ctrl+Alt+Delete with firecrackers & cucumbers
Navaratri		Goddess & Knowledge	Learning, Pause, Reset	One day where you're actually *forbidden* to study
Attukal Pongala		Women's Devotion	Sisterhood, Faith, Endurance	World's biggest women's cookout = divine feminism
Thrissur Pooram		Temple Spectacle	Unity, Style, Power	Elephants, beats, and fireworks that slap

🍚 INTERLUDE 6: THE PLATE PROTECTOR'S MANIFESTO—WHY I GUARD MY FOOD LIKE IT'S VIBRANIUM

I've got a weird flex and I'm not ashamed: **I don't share food**. Like, ever. What's on my plate is *mine*—not up for negotiation, sampling, or "just one bite" diplomacy.

Growing up in a big, lovable (and chaotic) Kerala Hindu family where food is practically a second religion, this made me a total anomaly. While others bonded over spoon-sharing and dosa diplomacy, I was the Po, kung-fu-gripping my dumplings like they were forged in Wakanda.

From a young age, I was the oddball who wouldn't touch another person's plate, nor let anyone near mine. My cousins made it their life's mission to troll me. Aunts engineered sneaky food ambushes like it was *SpongeBob's Prank Week*. Someone always "accidentally" dunked a vada in my sambar—like I wouldn't notice?

Only one soul had my back: my grandfather—the Dumbledore in a mundu—who'd say, "Leave the boy and his food alone," even as the whole extended fam giggled in the background.

Festivals, which should've meant feasting and fun, became battlegrounds where I'd dread the "communal eating experience." You haven't truly known anxiety until you've had to defend your banana chips at a group Onam sadhya like you are Steve Rogers facing down Thanos with a papadam.

🍵 Captain Rajiv Doesn't Share Food

Now that I am a full-grown adult (allegedly), the battlefield has simply shifted—from family feasts to work lunchrooms.

Colleagues at social hours, friends at parties, would all eye my plate or drink as if I am hoarding vibranium. (And I know they all do that only to annoy me)

"Wow! That looks delicious. Can I have just one bite?"

"Nope." Captain Rajiv has entered the chat.

I still get roasted harder than my Sunday beef fry.

One friend even gifted me a "Joey Doesn't Share Food" T-shirt—yes, from that old-school sitcom "Friends" (ask your parents). In that episode, Joey goes on a date and loses it when his date steals fries from his plate. I feel you, Joey!! Totallyyyy!!

Moral of the story? Joey doesn't share food. Neither do I.

Look—I get that for most people, sharing food = sharing love. But some of us are wired differently. Some heroes are willing to give up their entire plate, but please don't make them share. They eat it solo, with dignity and peace. And if that makes me the Loki of the lunch hour, so be it.

Just because I won't hand you a spoon doesn't mean I won't dish out culture. My food boundaries aren't a glitch—they are part of the cultural masala. Turns out, respecting someone's refusal to share papadam might be the most unexpectedly profound way to appreciate their heritage. So go ahead, feast on the traditions—but keep your fork on your side of the table.

CHAPTER 16:
PAINT, POISE & POWER:
FROM DANCE-OFF TO
DIVINE TAKEOVER
(The drama queens of Kerala)

Chapter 16: Paint, Poise, and Power: From Dance-Off to Divine Takeover

(The drama queens of Kerala)

Welcome to the ultimate spiritual showdown where Kerala's gods go full Hollywood, the eyebrows act harder than an Oscar snub, and the costumes scream louder than Thor dropping Mjölnir in a Kathakali temple. Grab your popcorn (or banana chips), because we're entering the holy multiverse of Kathakali, Mohiniyattam, and Theyyam—where storytelling meets spellcasting meets Beyoncé-level stage presence.

🎭 KATHAKALI: Avengers, But Make It Ancient and Eyeliner-Heavy

Imagine if Doctor Strange and Hulk fused into one character, dipped themselves in green paint, wore skirts the size of Hogwarts' dining hall tables, and told the Mahabharata using only facial muscles. That's Kathakali. Every glare is a mic drop. Every stomp is a cosmic boom.

And don't even get me started on the eye workouts —these dancers do more cardio with their pupils than most of us do with our entire bodies. The makeup? A color-coded myth chart: Green for hero, red for villain, black beard = BE VERY AFRAID.

The drums don't just play music. They attack your soul. Chenda beats hit like Hulk smashes—BAM —and suddenly, you're not watching a dance. You are inside a mythological Final Boss Fight.

💃 MOHINIYATTAM: The Elegant Assassin with Eyebrows Sharper Than Wanda's Comebacks

Mohiniyattam walks in like, "I could destroy you... gracefully." She is the cool, enchantress energy. Flowing white silk, gold borders, and the kind of eyebrow sass that could make even Voldemort blush.

It is Vishnu as a femme fatale, basically saying, "Watch me seduce demons and educate mortals—with minimal movement and maximum precision." The whole dance is one long, poetic eye roll, choreographed like a Slytherin duel — subtle, classy, lethal.

Each flick = flirtation. Each glance = emotional grenade. No backup dancers needed. This is a solo act. Just vibes, lighting, and enough control to summon cosmic grace on command.

🔥 THEYYAM: When the God Possesses You and Your Costume Has Wi-Fi Signal on the Moon

Now, Kathakali and Mohiniyattam are cool and all, but Theyyam? Theyyam kicks down the door like, "Yo, I *am* the god." Not playing. Not pretending. Legit possessed.

No stage. No chill. Theyyam arrives barefoot, with sky-high headgear, a face painted like a cosmic coloring book, and a fire circle that would give Ghost Rider FOMO. It is tradition meets trance meets straight-up divine possession.

The drummer's heartbeat. The crowd? Hushed. And suddenly—BAM—the divine is here, dancing through dust, flames, and dramatic slow-motion turns that would make even SpongeBob scream, "I'm ready... for transcendence!"

🏆 THE FINAL SHOWDOWN: Eyebrow Avengers Assemble

Who wins the divine dance-off? Trick question. YOU do.

Because when Kerala throws down spiritually, it is not about "winning." It's about vibing with forces older than Hogwarts, deeper than the Quantum Realm, and sassier than Kung Fu Panda's inner peace journey.

So next time someone says dance is "just an art form," raise a perfectly arched eyebrow and whisper:

"Tell that to my mudras, muggle." End scene.

🐫 Divine Dance-Off: One Page Field Guide 🐓🔥

💃 Dance Form / Element	📝 Description
☀ Kathakali = Thunder God Mode	Green face = hero, red = villain, black beard = run! Eyebrows do most of the talking. Chenda drums = boss battle soundtrack.
✨ Mohiniyattam = Enchanted Elegance	Vishnu's diva avatar sways and slays with slow motion sass. Every glance = backstory. Every tilt = emotional download.
🔥 Theyyam = Divine Rockstar Possession	No stage, no filter, just full-blown fire god vibes in a backyard ritual. Costume goal: frighten demons & dazzle humans.
👁 Mudras & Expressions = Language of the Gods	No words needed when your eyebrows are trained weapons and your hands tell epics.
🎬 Supernatural Line-Up	Avengers assemble? Nah. Kerala's got the triple threat — Stomp, Sway & Summon.
🙏 Cultural Combo Pack	One's thunder (Kathakali), one's lightning (Mohiniyattam), one's ritual wildfire (Theyyam). Together? They're the multiverse of movement.
💄 Style Points	From skirt-armor combos to flaming headgear to golden saree grace — this is haute divinity.
🏆 Moral of the Dance-Off	Real power isn't in your fists — it's in your pose, poise, and perfect pause.

CHAPTER 17:

KALARI RISING

TRAIN LIKE A SAGE, FIGHT LIKE A GUARDIAN

Chapter 17: Kalari Rising—Train Like a Sage, Fight Like a Guardian

Okay, real talk—this chapter hits close to home. While others geek out over baking shows or gaming, I have spent over 25 years in the martial arts world. One of the oldest and most powerful traditions? It is from my backyard: Kerala.

It is called Kalaripayattu—or Kalari. But don't expect slow-motion sword fights or fancy kicks alone. Kalari is a full-on lifestyle. It is spiritual, healing, and purposeful. It is the original warrior-sage path—built to protect Dharma.

Sanatana Dharma Isn't All Peace Signs and Hugs

People often reduce Hinduism to incense sticks and chill vibes. But Sanatana Dharma is about balance. Peace is sacred, yes—but when injustice rises, Dharma doesn't ask us to retreat. It asks us to rise.

This is where Shakti enters: divine strength that turns fear into courage. Not rage—righteous power. Like when your mom morphs into Durga with a rolling pin after someone insults your sibling.

Kalari = Shakti in Motion

Kalari embodies that, Shakti. But before stances, swords, or spin-kicks, there is the foundation: Guru-Shishya Parampara—India's ancient way of learning. No YouTube tutorials. You lived, breathed, and learned with your Guru.

🍫 The Four Pillars of Guru-Shishya Parampara

Like every other art form (music, dance), Kalari training followed a clear, powerful path:

- Shastra (The WHY): This is EXPLAINED. Philosophy and purpose. Moves mean nothing without context.
- Tantra (The HOW): This is TAUGHT. Technique—stance, breath, swing—mastered through repetition.
- Vidya (The REAL knowledge): This is PASSED DOWN. Wisdom earned through time and humility. Passed down, not downloaded.
- Kalā (The Art): This is DEVELOPED. Your spark. The unique flavor you bring.

Each pillar builds on the others. Skip one, and your path is incomplete. The Guru ties it all together—coach, guide, and walking library of wisdom.

Back to Kalari: The Warrior Monk's Path

Kalari is not about picking fights. It's about syncing body, mind, and spirit. Like the gods who bless with one hand and protect with the other—balance is everything.

You move with purpose, breathe with clarity, and train with respect. Not to dominate—but to stand with discipline and dignity.

The Origin Story:

Legend says Kalari began over 3,000 years ago with Parashurama, an avatar of Vishnu, who reclaimed land from the sea and founded 108 kalaris. Think ancient Jedi temples—Kerala style.

Even cooler? Shaolin Kung Fu may trace its roots back to Bodhidharma, a Kalari-trained monk who took this wisdom to China.

Inside a Kalari: More Than a Gym

Every Kalari is a sacred space, built with Vaastu principles and filled with meaning:

- Poothara: Honors deities and ancestors
- Guruthara: Respects the Guru
- Ankathattu: Duel/demo platform
- Vadivu: Animal-inspired stances (panther, cobra, elephant, etc.)

Kalari Levels: Your Spiritual RPG

Train as if you are leveling up in a cosmic video game:

1. Meipayattu—Body control: agility, breath, awareness
2. Kolthari—Wooden weapons: staffs, sticks
3. Ankathari—Metal weapons: swords, spears, urumi (whip-sword!)
4. Verumkai—Empty-hand combat: locks, strikes, grapples

Each lesson includes bows, breathwork, and reverence. The fight is never just physical—it is spiritual.

Training That Heals, Not Just Hurts

Kalari pairs beautifully with Ayurveda for total wellness:

- Marma therapy: Energy point healing
- Herbal oil massages: For strength and recovery
- Yoga and rehab: For resilience and flow

You rise by refining your spirit and restoring your body.

Meenakshi Amma Gurukkal—The OG Kalari Avenger

If Kalari had Avengers, Meenakshi Amma would be the desi Black Widow — ageless, fierce, and wise. At over 80, she still kicks high and spins swords at Kadathanadan Kalari Sangam in Vadakara, Kerala.

While most grandmas offer unniyappams, she delivers leg sweeps and life lessons.

She's living proof that true power doesn't retire—it just gets sharper.

Kalari's Comeback Story

Colonial rulers tried to suppress Kalari—too powerful, too rooted, too uncolonizable. But it never died. It just waited.

Long before capes and CGI, there was Thacholi Othenan, a Kalari legend whose skills became folklore. So unbeatable, it took a bullet to stop him. Swords weren't enough.

Now? Kalari is back—globally.

- Used in Indian military training
- Featured in cinematic stunts
- Adapted for therapy and movement

And leading the charge?

Vidyut Jammwal—Bollywood action star, real-life martial artist, and Kalari ambassador. Grace, strength, purpose—and some serious kicks.

⚖️ Final Takeaway:

Train with Purpose. Defend with Dharma.

Let Meenakshi Amma remind you:

- Age is just a number
- Power is a mindset
- Dharma is your training ground

To protect Dharma is Dharma.

You don't need an armor to be a warrior. You need:

- A clear mind
- A strong body
- A grounded spirit
- The courage to act

Whether you are standing up to bullies, training in combat, or just showing up for your people—

You carry Shakti. Train like a sage. Fight like a guardian.

Now,

Bow. Breathe. Begin.

Chapter 18:
The Comeback Code
From Spelling Bees to Dharmic Fight Club

Chapter 18: The Comeback Code —From Spelling Bees to Dharmic Fight Club

🐝 **Dear millennial and Gen Z Hindu (and honorary spiritual sidekicks),**

Let's be real. You have been crushing spelling bees since you could spell "onomatopoeia." Your GPA glows like Tony Stark's Arc Reactor, and your SAT score probably alerted NASA.

Remember Tae Kwon Do? You kicked air for two years, snagged that black belt (Asian Parent Approved™), and never looked back. Another checkbox ✔ between Kumon, STEM, and coding camp.

Somewhere between PSAT prep and piano recitals, we stopped moving like warriors and started sitting like spreadsheets.

🛡 Where Did Our Inner Warrior Go?

We traded dharma for deadlines. In chasing gold medals, we dropped the golden mean.

But here's the plot twist: Our ancestors weren't just spiritual—they were battle-tested.

- Vishwamitra meditated hard enough to crack the cosmos.
- Bhishma took a vow that made even Thor flinch.
- Karna had loyalty that would make Captain America cry.
- Krishna made diplomacy look cooler than espionage.

They weren't quiet achievers. They were cosmic multitools:

- Chanakya brain + Arjuna aim + Hanuman heart.

And then... we became model immigrants. Polite. Apologetic. Sometimes, painfully passive.

We forgot: Sanatana Dharma isn't submission. It's balance.

Yes, we meditate but we are also meant to defend.

Yes, we chant but we are also meant to train.

What Would Po Do?

Master Shifu didn't choose Po for his muscles.

He chose him because Po showed up. Fell. Got up again. Trained. Between dumplings and destiny, he became the Dragon Warrior. You can too.

⧗ It's Comeback Time

You don't need a Kalari school to become a warrior. It is not the style — it is the discipline.

Boxing. Karate. MMA. Krav Maga. Even Tai Chi. Anything. If it hones your breath, your focus, your courage, it's on the path.

Go back to that old TKD school if you want. Not to get another silly black belt in 2 years, but to "become" one over time.

⚔ Your Comeback Code

Mix:

- Chanakya strategy
- Spider-man reflexes
- Krishna calmness
- Iron man grit

And one last ingredient…

⚡ The Final Upgrade

- You are not training to become a hero.
- You are training because you already are one.
- You are not a bystander with opinions.
- You are the warrior we have been waiting for.

🕉 Spoiler alert: The Kalki prophecy?

It is not just about a sword-wielding rider on a horse.

It is about you—waking up.

CHAPTER 19:

KALKI IS YOU

- AWAKENING THE HINDU THIS AGE NEEDS

Chapter 19: Kalki Is You
—Awakening the Hindu This Age Needs

"Not all heroes ride white horses. Some just update their firmware and get to work."

This chapter isn't about mythology. It is about accountability. It is about waking up to the reality that the Kalki you're waiting for—the one who will protect Dharma, restore balance, and fight back against adharma—has already arrived. And it is you.

Wake-Up Spell: *Expecto Self-Responsibility! *

Once upon a recent time in Pahalgam, peaceful people were targeted just for being Hindu. No wands, no weapons, no warning. They trusted Karma to auto-defend like a magical shield. But guess what?

Karma doesn't do passive mode. And Shakti needs you to do your part.

Let that sink in! These are not Hogwarts spells. You've got to cast it yourself.

Bhakti ≠ Blind Mode

Being Hindu isn't about sitting silently like a yogi on airplane mode. Shakti isn't a fantasy power-up. It doesn't just flow; you've got to train, focus, and use it! You can't just chant and chill.

Chanakya vs Chill Mode

Chanakya wasn't in a cave humming mantras while empires fell. Arjuna didn't win by reciting shlokas. He picked up the bow, looked injustice in the eye, and went full Avengers Assemble.

Mirror, Mirror, Who's the Avatar?

Still waiting for a white horse guy? Sorry, this isn't a Marvel end-credit scene. Kalki isn't up in the clouds doing pushups. He/She is in your reflection. That righteous rage you feel when truth gets mocked? That's your *Dharma-sense tingling*, like Peter Parker before the chaos.

New Age Hindu = Mantra + Muscles

You want to protect Dharma? Get spiritually swole. Train your mind (read up, wise up), train your voice (speak up), train your body (with whatever suits your superhero origin story).

⚠️ Get this (again):

No one is coming to save you. When violence comes calling, will you be ready with something? Or go down with nothing but awesome SAT scores and spelling bee medals?

Silence Is Not Gold. It's Adharma

Being quiet while your culture is dragged, your people are attacked, and your beliefs are mocked? That is not calmness. That's cowardice with a spiritual filter. Even SpongeBob screams when Plankton shows up with another evil plan. Speak. Up.

Peace Without Power = A Pause Button

If you think Dharma is just about being peaceful, remember: peace without power is just surrender with better PR. It is like putting Thanos in timeout. It won't work.

Final Quest: Download the Kalki Update

This chapter isn't a rage-fueled rant. It is a rally cry for a new generation of Hindus who don't just wear tilaks and quote verses but who *stand* for something. You have inherited a Dharma full of poetry, power, and precision. Now upgrade it with your voice, your courage, your conscience. Be fierce like Devi. Be aware like Shiva. Be wise like Yudhishthira. Be ready like Hanuman. Kalki isn't coming. **Kalki is you.**

⊘ Field Guide: "Kalki.exe Activated"

	Icon	What It Means
1	🪔	Look in the mirror. Yep, it's on you now.
2	🧠	Chanakya mode: Smart is the new spiritual.
3	⚔️	Arjuna mode: Fight, but with purpose.
4	🧘	Daily training: mantra, motion, mission.
5	🗣️	Speak truth, not just memes.
6	🛑	Stop being silent. Start standing up.
7	🔥	Rage for Dharma, not drama.

Section 6:

Wrap-Up and Beyond

CONCLUSION:
THE CHAIN MUST NOT BREAK

⊘ Conclusion: The Chain Must Not Break

Our ancestors preserved Dharma against all odds. Now it is our turn to live it, guard it, and pass it on.

Why Do We Lose Our Roots So Easily?

I came across an article that listed five reasons Hindus are quick to abandon their roots and convert to other faiths:

- Weak connection with Dharma
- Absence of direction, causing spiritual confusion
- Lack of strong communal bonds, making it easy to drift away
- Difficulty understanding Dharma in the absence of regular guidance from parents and elders
- Misunderstanding the purpose of worship and the role of temples

These are not minor issues. They are cracks in the foundation. And when the ground shakes, it's no surprise that many walk away. Such vulnerabilities, when cleverly exploited, lead to easy conversion.

The Roots Matter More Than the Rituals

Here's the truth: when roots are shallow, even a small storm can topple the tree. Too often we carry the label of Hindu without the lived wisdom. We know the festivals but forget their essence. We inherit the rituals but rarely understand their depth.

That's why "simpler" logics from other traditions feel tempting. They seem clearer only because we abandoned the clarity that was already ours.

Our ancestors lived, fought, and died to preserve Sanatana Dharma. The least we can do is live it — so the chain is never broken.

Old Traditions, New Questions

Lighting a nilavilakku today might trigger a motion sensor or get you photobombed by the cat. But the how is not the point — the why is.

The younger generations aren't rejecting rituals; they're asking, "Why?" And when the answers are thoughtful — rooted in meaning, science, or symbolism — they stop being empty habits and start becoming compelling practices.

- Pradakshina becomes cosmic alignment, not empty circling.
- Fasting becomes discipline and empathy, not hunger games.
- Mantras become sound-technology for the mind, not mumbling syllables.

Sanatana Dharma is not fragile. It has survived millennia, not by force or conversion, but by depth, flexibility, and inner strength. The weakness lies not in the tradition — but in our awareness of it.

A Call to Deepen

The solution isn't guilt or blind following. It's study. Reflection. Exploration. Living the questions until they become answers.

When we do this, we don't just preserve a culture — we turn it into living wisdom. And when we pass that on, we give our children more than identity. We give them roots no storm can break.

Final Thought

Sanatana Dharma doesn't ask you to follow blindly. It invites you to understand, to practice, to live. To know that every lamp lit, every verse recited, every act of kindness is part of a tradition older than history yet alive in you today.

If you carry it with awareness and pride, you won't need to defend it. It will defend itself — through you.

The chain must not break — because you are the next link.

🔥 CLOSING REFLECTION: THE LAMP AND THE FLAME

A lamp by itself is just metal and wick.

It is the flame that gives it meaning.

In the same way, rituals, stories, and festivals are only forms — beautiful, yes, but empty without understanding. It is the flame of awareness, the spark of lived wisdom, that turns them into light.

Sanatana Dharma has carried this flame for thousands of years — through kingdoms and colonies, temples and battlefields, victories and defeats. It has never demanded conquest. It has only asked to be remembered, renewed, and passed on.

Now the lamp is in your hands.

Light it with questions.

Protect it with learning.

Share it with pride.

And carry it forward so that, long after us, it will still burn — quietly, steadily, eternally.

Appendix I: 5 Hindu Legends Who Slayed in Science, Math, Medicine, Lit, and War

Subtitle: *When Desis Went Full Avengers Mode (Without the CGI Budget)*

Not all heroes wear capes. Some wore dhotis, scribbled on palm leaves, and dropped truth bombs so powerful they still echo through labs, libraries, and launchpads today.

Here is your spiritual snack pack of five legendary Hindu minds who leveled up humanity—no filter, no Wi-Fi, just pure brilliance and occasional plot armor.

1. Aryabhata (c. 476 CE)—The OG Mathlete with Universe-Sized Brainpower

Field: Math and Astronomy

Hogwarts Title: Head of Ravenclaw + Divination Professor

Calculated π, figured out Earth spins, and launched heliocentric vibes before Copernicus.

Invented zero. Basically, built the foundation of modern science with a scroll and brainpower.

Modern Marvel equivalent: Tony Stark with a trigonometry obsession.

2. Sushruta (c. 600 BCE)—The Surgeon Supreme of Ancient India

Field: Medicine and Surgery

Kung Fu Panda Title: Master of Scalpels and Sutras

Wrote the Sushruta Samhita—300+ surgical procedures, 120 instruments, and the OG nose job manual.

Spiritual superpower: Ayurvedic Jedi skills.

Marvel match-up: Doctor Strange but with neem oil and a scalpel.

3. Kalidasa (c. 4th–5th century CE)—The Literary Sorcerer with a Pen Sharper Than a Chakra

Field: Literature and Poetry

Harry Potter Vibe: The Desi Shakespeare meets Dumbledore with a poetic Patronus

Master of Sanskrit drama and nature-driven verse. His plays and poems could make even Krishna blush.

Modern equivalent: Lin-Manuel Miranda x Rumi in a lotus pose.

4. Chanakya (c. 4th century BCE)—The Grandmaster of Strategy and Sass

Field: Politics, Economics, Warfare

Game of Thrones Title: Desi Tyrion Lannister with Ashram Access

Wrote the Arthashastra—spy networks, political hacks, and economic wisdom.

Icon status: Empire whisperer and intellectual hitman.

Marvel equivalent: Nick Fury meets Loki (less mischief, more mission).

5. Chhatrapati Shivaji Maharaj (1630–1680 CE)—Mountain Lion with a Mullet and a Mission

Field: Warfare and Leadership

Marvel Vibe: Captain America meets Black Panther with a dash of desi swag

The unstoppable force behind the Maratha Empire. Rose from jagir to juggernaut using brains over brawn, mountain fortresses like Rajgad and Raigad, and hit-and-run tactics that gave Mughal generals nightmares. Escaped house arrest using next-level parkour and cloak-and-dagger drama.

Established Hindu self-rule with tolerance for all faiths, a disciplined army/navy, and a code of ethics fit for a king. Crowned himself in a Sanskrit coronation to revive swarajya pride.

Legacy: Guerrilla GOAT, master strategist, and the OG desi freedom fighter.

Modern mash-up: Batman in a turban + Mission: Impossible + Dharma-coded justice.

Special Mention:

Ahalyabai Holkar: The Temple Rebuilder Supreme

If India had its own Avengers lineup of legendary rulers, Ahalyabai Holkar would be our version of Pepper Potts meets Wonder Woman— classy, fierce, and getting stuff done while the rest were busy flexing in sabhas and swinging swords.

In an age when widows were expected to disappear behind veils and vanish from public life like Jedi in exile, Ahalyabai picked up her metaphorical broomstick (or maybe Mjölnir?) and ruled Indore like an absolute boss.

But wait—she didn't stop at ruling. This queen went on a full-scale temple restoration mission across India like a magical quest in Zelda. Her side missions? Not hunting horcruxes—but rebuilding the dharma map of India by restoring sacred sites that had been destroyed or neglected over centuries of invasions and chaos.

Enter Kashi Vishwanath—Shiva's OG Chill Spot

The Kashi Vishwanath Temple in Varanasi (also known as Lord Shiva's bachelor pad in the spiritual multiverse) had been razed multiple times by invading Muslim rulers. By the 1700s, it was a shadow of its former glory—torn down, trampled, and turned into rubble.

That's when Ahalyabai rolled in—not with an army, but with gold, grit, and massive civil planning skills. In 1780, she rebuilt the temple next to the original ruins with grace, not vengeance. While the Mughal tyrant Aurangzeb had turned part of the old temple into the Gyanvapi mosque, Ahalyabai chose not to demolish it—because her vibe was peace, not politics.

With no Twitter threads or government aid, she funded and built:

- A brand-new Kashi Vishwanath Temple complex
- Roads, ghats, dharmashalas (traveler inns), and water tanks around it
- Pilgrim-friendly spaces for everyone, no caste cards needed

She did for Shiva what Tony Stark did for Peter Parker—gave him a home base, a suit-up spot, and some serious respect.

But wait—there's more!

She also rebuilt Somnath, Rameswaram, Gaya, Omkareshwar, and dozens more temples like a pan-India dharma architect. Her blueprint? Oneness, access, and dignity for all who walk the path of Sanatana Dharma. No loud politics. Just quiet, powerful seva.

Legacy Vibes

While modern leaders debate temple policies, Ahalyabai did the work centuries ago—without fanfare, without fundraisers, and without playing the victim. She didn't need viral reels—her temples are still standing.

If Shiva had a "Most Valuable Bhakt" plaque in Kailasa, this queen would be on it—right next to Nandi and the guy who invented rudraksha beads.

TL; DR?

Ahalyabai Holkar: The Gandalf of temple restoration, and the spiritual CEO India didn't know it needed—until she rewrote the map of devotion with a chisel, a checkbook, and a whole lot of chutzpah.

APPENDIX II: 5 LEGENDS WHO SHOOK UP KERALA

(And Didn't Wait for Instagram to Go Viral)

Subtitle: From spiritual rebels to hugging saints, here are five iconic humans who left Kerala (and Hindu society) a little wiser, braver, and a lot more woke.

1. Sree Narayana Guru (1855–1928)

The OG Equality Influencer

This man dropped truth bombs way before hashtags. His slogan? "One caste, one religion, one God for all." Boom—mic drop.

He told an entire society to quit obsessing over birth-based hierarchies and start treating humans like, well, humans. He led reforms, opened temples to all, and basically dragged Kerala toward spiritual equality—one wise verse at a time.

2. V.T. Bhattathiripad (1896–1982)

The Brahmin Who Canceled Brahminical Privilege—Before It Was Cool

Born into a strict Namboothiri household, V.T. Bhattathiripad busted out with wit, stage plays, and social critique.

Think of him as a 20th-century mic-dropping playwright who said, "Enough with the myths, already."

He used drama and satire to roast outdated customs and champion reform—from widow remarriage to temple access. If Kerala had a Netflix back then, this guy would've had a hit series and a stand-up special.

3. Mata Amritanandamayi (1953–)

The Hug That Went Global

A spiritual powerhouse with one superpower: the infinite hug.

People call her Amma—and she has hugged literally millions around the world. But she is not just about warm fuzzies. She built hospitals, schools, disaster relief teams, and a spiritual empire out of compassion and action.

Her Ashram at Amritapuri? Think Hogwarts—but for peace, purpose, and occasional bhajans.

4. Swami Chinmayananda (1916–1993)

The Vedanta Vlogger (Before Wi-Fi Was Invented)

Swami C turned high-octane Hindu philosophy into something you could actually understand without an existential breakdown.

He made the Upanishads binge-worthy, hosted talks that filled halls, and started the Chinmaya Mission, which now spans the globe.

If you ever thought Vedanta was "too deep"—this guy was the friendly translator, meme-free but unforgettable.

5. K. Kelappan (1889–1971)

The Kerala Gandhi (except much better than G-man, and with a more genuine stance)

Kelappan wasn't here for caste nonsense. He led the Vaikom Satyagraha—a protest that basically said, "Let people walk on roads and enter temples, please."

A freedom fighter with peaceful vibes, he blended Hindu ethics with no-nonsense activism.

Wore khadi, fought prejudice, and stood up for the marginalized. Respect.

Bottom Line:

These five legends didn't just pray—they protested, preached, hugged, wrote, taught, and changed Kerala's spiritual DNA forever. No filters. Just fierce compassion and unfiltered reform.

APPENDIX III: FIVE THINGS HINDUS CAN TOTALLY FLEX ABOUT (AND SHOULD)

Subtitle: Why Your Culture Deserves a Mic Drop—With Mantras

Let's be honest—between WhatsApp forwards, endless news debates, and your uncle's unsolicited hot takes, Hinduism often gets reduced to either a nostalgic curry ad or a chaotic meme war. But peel back the drama, and what you will find is a cultural treasure chest so deep, even Indiana Jones would need backup.

So here it is: Five solid reasons Hindus can (and should) puff their chest a little—no arrogance, just ancestral awesomeness.

1. Time? We Invented It. (Also, We've Been Here Forever)

Other cultures: "Our history goes back 2,000 years!"

Hinduism: "That's adorable."

The Rig Veda is over 3,500 years old—and that's just what we have dated with science. Our timelines don't just go back centuries—they go back yugas, cosmic cycles that make the Marvel multiverse look like fan fiction.

We were tracking eclipses, calculating planetary orbits, and philosophizing about consciousness when most civilizations were still arguing over fire.

TL; DR: We didn't just mark time. We made time nervous.

2. Dharma: The OG Moral Operating System

Before anyone trademarked "mindfulness" or TED-talked about "ethical leadership," we had Dharma—a concept so flexible and powerful it can apply to kings, carpenters, cats, and K-dramas (okay, maybe not cats).

Dharma isn't just "doing the right thing." It is a custom-fitted spiritual GPS that recalibrates based on your role, time, and situation. Your vibe, your duties, your choices—it is all built in.

TL; DR: It is the reason Arjuna didn't rage-quit the Mahabharata.

3. Diversity is Our Default Setting

Monocultures are boring. Hinduism is a spiritual buffet.

- Want one god? We've got you.
- Many gods? Sure!
- No god, just cosmic law? Totally valid.
- Prefer philosophy to rituals? Welcome to the Upanishads.
- Into singing, dancing, and full-blown drama? Say hello to Bhakti.

From Shaivism to Shaktism, Dvaita to Advaita, we have got more schools of thought than Hogwarts has houses—and guess what? They are all somehow friends (or frenemies).

TL; DR: Unity in diversity? We practically trademarked it.

4. Spiritual Swag with Zero Gatekeeping

Yoga. Ayurveda. Meditation. Mantras. Temple architecture that doubles as cosmic maps.

And the best part? We didn't gatekeep.

Hindu knowledge systems crossed oceans without missionaries or marketing plans. People came looking for it—whether it was for a cure, a guru, or inner peace (or a vacation in Rishikesh).

We've been offering "healing and higher consciousness" way before it was made a business model.

TL; DR: Our export list includes more than just spices.

5. Rebellion is in Our Bloodline

Yes, there are problems—past and present. But guess what?

Every time we got too rigid, someone inside the system pulled out the spiritual screwdriver and said, "Time for an upgrade."

- Buddha? Total Hindu soft uninstaller of caste rigidity.
- Ambedkar said, "No more untouchability—deal with it."
- Bhakti poets? Called out the elite in verse form (with rhythm and sass).
- V.T. Bhattathiripad? Roasted Puranas harder than Twitter ever could.

Hinduism isn't static—it evolves, which is probably why it's still alive and kicking, thousands of years in.

TL; DR: We reform like pros. With poetry, protests, and the occasional flaming trident.

Final Thought: 🌀

So next time someone asks, "Why are you proud to be Hindu?"

Don't just shrug and say, "Because Amma said so."

Say: "Because our timelines are cosmic, our traditions are layered, our teachings are timeless, and our gods have better costumes than Marvel"

And also, because:

We are the only people who bow to the sun, pray to the river, dance with the gods, question them, feed them payasam —then recycle the banana.

That is our culture. That is our chaos. That is our home.

Appendix IV: Sadhya, Sacred Snacks, and Coma Karma:

Kerala's Divine Dining Experience: From leaf-loaded lunch buffets to desserts so good even the gods do a double-take.

Sadhya: The OG Banana Leaf Buffet of Kerala

If Kerala had a superhero meal, it would be Sadhya—a massive, colorful, flavor-packed feast served on a banana leaf. You don't just eat a Sadhya. You experience it. Weddings? Sadhya. Onam? Sadhya. Housewarming? Temple festival? Tuesday, that feels like a celebration? You guessed it—Sadhya.

This isn't your average lunch. It's a sacred ritual of gratitude, generosity, and serious stomach-stretching. And the best part? It's completely vegetarian but somehow still feels like a food festival in your mouth.

Why a Banana Leaf, Though?

Let's address the giant green plate in the room. Yes, the food is served on an actual banana leaf. Why?

Because:

- It is 100% eco-friendly ♻️ (our ancestors did zero waste before it was cool).
- The leaf adds a subtle flavor 🌿 (like a culinary Snapchat filter).
- It is wide, waterproof, and naturally antibacterial 🛡️ (basically, the green iPad of food presentation).
- In Ayurveda, it is considered pure and cooling ❄️.

Also, let's be honest—there is something satisfying about eating off a giant leaf while sitting on the floor like royalty from 200 BC.

The Sadhya Layout: Organized Chaos on a Leaf

There is an art to arranging a Sadhya. You can't just throw stuff on the leaf and hope for the best. Each item has a specific place, taste, and purpose—and when done right, it is like a perfectly choreographed food flash mob.

Here is the typical flow:

Top row, left to right (a.k.a. the Avengers Assemble lineup):

- Upperi—Banana chips (snack goals)
- Sharkara Varatti—Sweet jaggery banana chips
- Pickles—Mango, lime (tiny explosions of tangy chaos)
- Pachadi and Kichadi—Yogurt-based dishes
- Olan—Coconut milk magic with ash gourd
- Avial—Veggies wearing a coconut-yogurt coat
- Thoran—Stir-fried vegetables with coconut
- Kootu Curry—Chickpeas + yam = comfort food
- Erissery—Pumpkin + coconut curry = happiness
- Pulissery—Buttermilk curry that's slightly sour and seriously soothing

Center of the leaf (a.k.a. The Main Event):

- Steamed Kerala red rice—fluffy, earthy, and filling
- Parippu (dal), Sambar, and Rasam—your three-stage gravy mission, from thick to thin to drinkable

Sweet stuff (a.k.a. Dessert Heaven):

- Payasam, Ada Pradhaman, Palada—sweet, soupy puddings
- Served with pappadam (giant crispy cracker) and maybe a banana

Everything is eaten with the right hand—yes, that's part of the tradition. (Don't worry, you get the hang of it quickly… just don't wear white.)

The Banana Leaf Fold Test: How to Say "Thanks" Without Saying It

Once you're full and emotionally bonded with your payasam, you fold the banana leaf. But wait—it matters how you fold it, and this is debatable because both versions exist. However, the popular practice seems to be as follows:

- Fold it toward you = "Chef's kiss! That was awesome." (This is the usual, polite way.)
- Fold it away from you = "Meh. I'm not impressed." (Usually saved for sad occasions or, you know, funerals.)

So yeah, even your leaf gets to speak for you. Because Kerala doesn't do subtle.

🌈 Conclusion: A Leaf, A Meal, A Whole Mood

Sadhya is way more than just a festive lunch. It is a flavor map of Kerala, a celebration of balance, and proof that vegetarian food can be a full-on flavor party 🎆. Every dish in the Sadhya represents a different taste—sweet, salty, bitter, sour, pungent, astringent—just like life.

It is about community, culture, connection, and yes, a fair amount of burping with pride afterward.

So next time you see a banana leaf being unrolled, clear your schedule, wear stretchy pants, and prepare your tastebuds 😋. Sadhya isn't just a meal—it is a tradition you can taste.

Holy Snacks, Batman! Unniyappam and Palada Payasam— The Deity-Approved Dessert Drop

Look, I've saved this section for last for a reason. Not because it is "least important," but because, well... we've reached dessert. And as any wise person or well-fed deity will tell you: you don't rush dessert.

Kerala temples are not just spiritual hotspots—they are flavor zones. Each one comes with its own signature prasadam; a divine snack blessed by the gods and powered by tradition, prayer, and possibly grandmother-level cooking secrets.

Let's talk about the GOATs of the temple treat world:

Unniyappam: The Original Divine Donut (and My Personal Prasadam Crush)

Small, round, fried, and sweet enough to make your eyes roll back in bliss—unniyappam is basically Kerala's holy pancake ball. Made with banana, jaggery, rice flour, and love (plus oil. *So much oil*), it is crispy outside, soft inside, and 100% "Can I have three more, please?"

Personally, this one is my forever favorite. Growing up, I'd fight for the last one in the prasadam bowl like it was the final Infinity Stone. Even now, no matter how spiritual the moment, I'll admit—if there is unniyappam on the plate, my soul might be focused, but my stomach is leading the meditation.

You will find these blessed bundles at temples like:
- Sri Krishna Temple, Ambalappuzha
- Kumaranalloor Bhagavathi Temple
- Or occasionally in your dreams if you've been really good

Legend says even the gods don't say no to unniyappam. And neither should you.

Palada Payasam: The Royal Liquid Gold

Enter: Palada Payasam—Kerala's answer to "What if milk and rice had a glow-up?"

Creamy, silky, slow-cooked rice pudding with cardamom-scented elegance and just enough sweetness to forgive everyone for everything.

Divine Calories, Infinite Blessings

These aren't just snacks. These are prasadam—meaning they've been offered to the deity first. So yes, that unniyappam is charged with sacred energy, and that palada? It is practically a spiritual smoothie.

Consuming prasadam is like the universe saying:

"You've done well, young devotee. Now eat." You are not just eating food—you are part of a cosmic exchange program of devotion, blessings, and mild food comas.

Spiritual Takeaway:

You've fasted. You've chanted. You've walked barefoot across scorching flagstones. And now? Now, you feast—on Unniyappam, Palada Payasam, and Pure Joy.

Pssst: Just make sure to get your own plate and not to touch mine!

Honestly, if all spiritual practices ended with carbs and sugar, we'd all be sages by now.

Final Thought: 🌀 The Karma of Coma: Sadhya, Sleep, and Superpowers

Ever wonder why Indian households treat afternoon naps like a sacred ritual?

Simple: Sadhya + Palada Payasam = Instant coma. Harry Potter had his Invisibility Cloak; we have banana leaves that make you vanish into a food coma by 3 p.m. sharp.

And here's the killer move: Every trip to Kerala makes me 10 lbs heavier—minimum. One glorious sadhya has enough calories to make your calorie counter quit in protest.

I like to think of it as training: I gain now so I can *Avengers Assemble* later at the gym. Basically, I earn a month's worth of workouts in one tasty, turmeric-drenched sitting.

Moral of the story? Come for the culture, stay for the food, and clear your post-lunch schedule.

Appendix V: Dharma Download— Final Life Hacks

(Because enlightenment should come with bullet points)

1. Ask "Why," Not Just "How"

If a ritual feels weird or outdated, don't just follow—investigate. Respect doesn't mean robot mode.

2. Culture ≠ Costume Party

Tradition isn't about blindly copying—it is about understanding the why behind the what. Know it, own it, remix it with intent.

3. Caste ≠ Character

Judge people by their values, not their varna. Dharma never endorsed discrimination—humans added that bug later.

4. Temple Tantrums Happen

If the deity's seat sparks more debates than the budget, don't worry—you're not alone. The divine has seen worse.

5. Superstition ≠ Spirituality

Milk going bad doesn't mean the gods are mad. Maybe check the fridge before blaming the universe, or in some cases, invest in a fridge instead of relying on tropical cooling.

6. Reform is Holy Too

Ctrl + Alt + Dharma: Sometimes, rebooting the system is the most sacred thing you can do.

7. Make Your Own Festival Manual

Don't wait for tradition to knock. Start your own family rituals. Light a lamp. Tell a story. Celebrate with snacks. Film a family reel, maybe?

8. Sanskrit Optional, Sincerity Mandatory

Chant if you want, stumble through it if you must—but do it with heart.

9. Keep the Flame, Drop the Fuss

You can love your culture and laugh at its absurdities. That is how you keep it real and alive.

10. Always Leave the Door Open—for Curiosity

Whether it is a temple, a text, or a tantric mystery, don't lock yourself into dogma. Keep asking. Keep wondering. The gods can handle it.

🧘 Final Thought:

There is no one-size-fits-all path. Just find your light—and walk with it.

 ABOUT THE AUTHOR

https://hashtaghindu.com

Not a Guru. Not a Podcaster. Definitely Not Your Typical WhatsApp Uncle.

The author is a middle-aged, globe-trotting Indian American engineer-businessman, who's somehow managed to juggle martial arts, fitness, music, parenting, and existential crises with a mix of grace, sweat, and a lot of rice, pappadam, and reflection.

He lives somewhere between time zones and timeless questions—often found on a trans-Atlantic flight pondering the cosmos, or in a home gym wondering if Advaita Vedanta supports cheat days. Holding black belts in Jujitsu and Kempo Karate, he is also the kind of dad who quotes both Bruce Lee and the Upanishads—usually in the same breath—right before reminding you to brush your teeth "with awareness."

Not a fan of the filter-heavy, hashtag-chasing brand of cultural organizations, he has spent decades quietly rolling his eyes at their theatrics—preferring instead to nerd out on history, sink into books, question everything, and explore Sanatana Dharma on his own terms. Preferably barefoot. Preferably near a temple hall with excellent acoustics.

This book wasn't in the plans. Not until the gods—or possibly boredom during biweekly transatlantic flights—tossed him a cosmic writing prompt. For years, he believed he'd only publish once he figured out whether he was agnostic, atheist, or just allergic to labels. But clarity is overrated, and the next generation wasn't going to wait.

So here it is part spiritual decoder, part history remix, and entirely driven by a desire to reconnect roots, clean off the dogma, and pass on the good stuff—without guilt-tripping anyone in the process.

He continues to read avidly, train in martial arts obsessively, learn Tabla and Hindustani vocal music diligently, and question everything more regularly than he takes naps. And no, he still hasn't figured it all out—but that is kind of the point.

"I didn't choose the dharmic life. The dharmic life showed up while I was trying to stream cricket matches at odd hours on long flights with poor Wi-Fi."

📊 Sidebar Stats

- Spiritual Weakness: Overthinks everything. Including the quantity of prasad.
- Current Status: Still unsure if he's spiritually single or just in a complicated situationship with the universe.

www.ingramcontent.com/pod-product-compliance
Lightning Source LLC
Chambersburg PA
CBHW051609120626
46551CB00014B/1729